Chosen ... To Never Walk Alone!

An Inspiring Story of a Disabled
Christian Woman's Life

Susan J. Shanks, Ph.D.

Inspiring Voices®
A Service of **Guideposts**

Inspiring Voices books may be ordered through booksellers or by contacting:

Inspiring Voices
1663 Liberty Drive
Bloomington, IN 47403
www.inspiringvoices.com
1-(866) 697-5313

Scripture quotations marked (NIV) are taken from the HOLY BIBLE, NEW INTERNATIONAL VERSION ®. Copyright © 1973, 1978, 1984 by International Bible Society. Used by permission of Zondervan Publishing House. All rights reserved.

Scripture quotations marked (TLB) are taken from The Living Bible Copyright © 1971. Used by permission of Tyndale House Publishers, Inc., Wheaton, Illinois 60189. All rights reserved.

ISBN: 978-1-4624-0480-3 (sc)
ISBN: 978-1-4624-0479-7 (e)

Library of Congress Control Number: 2012923770

Printed in the United States of America

Inspiring Voices rev. date: 1/30/2013

Also by Susan J. Shanks

The HOPE Series

Facing Death with HOPE,
Haciendo frente a la muerte con ESPERANZA,
Prayers for Seniors,
Blessings for Sunrise to Sunrise,
Facing Grief with HOPE,
Haciendo frente al duelo con ESPERANZA,
Facing Life's Trials with HOPE

AND

House of Angels:
Living Independently
with a Family of In-Home Caregivers

For my family of relatives, friends and caregivers.

"You did not choose me,
but I chose you
to go and bear fruit..."
JOHN 15.16 (NIV)

Table of Contents

Foreword

FROM THE TIME I JOINED the faculty at FSU in August, 1979, I was both impressed with and curious about the influence Susan Shanks exerted over many people at the university and off-campus. Pondering her unique range and depth of influence, I discovered the source in a personal conversation I had with her one day.

We were discussing how *"we are God's workmanship, created in Christ Jesus to do good works, which God prepared in advance for us to do"* (Eph. 2.10).

As we talked about how we both were God's workmanship, masterpieces with specially designed purposes, I realized how Susan's awareness of this truth has shaped her life and interactions with others.

Through Susan, God teaches, inspires, delights and encourages, informs and uplifts all who are blessed to have their life in some way intersect with hers. God, as the Master Artist, has as His primary concern the desire to express Himself--His thoughts and His intentions--through what He has crafted from each of our lives. Susan's awareness of this desire and her willingness to place herself fully in His Potter's hands has enabled Him to bless many of us who know and love her so well.

Perhaps through this book, God will choose to widen even more Susan's sphere of influence. May you, the reader, carry away from this book lessons Susan has learned and be given a fresh perspective on how God takes all situations and circumstances in a person's life, good and bad, and orchestrates them as part of a great chorus meant to glorify Himself – overabundantly blessing the vessels He has chosen in the process.

Paul W. Ogden, Ph.D., Professor Emeritus,
California State University, Fresno
Department of Communicative
Disorders and Deaf Studies

How? What? Who?
When? Why?

IN THIS BOOK I THANK God for His infinite patience while He lovingly prepared me to serve Him during my *golden years*. I am grateful to those who played an important role in molding me to fit into God's plan. They will, I believe, receive their reward from Him for their service to me.

What events in my life prepared me to serve God? How long did it take to educate me for His work? I began to answer these questions late in life.

My first attempts to recall my past began in 1995, shortly after the death of my mother – my closest and dearest friend and lifetime caregiver. Mother and the Lord had carried me through the illness which left me with almost complete paralysis of every muscle of my body except those of my face. They guided me during the years when I prepared for a career, and they supported me the thirty years plus when I worked as a speech pathologist and university professor. I had completed my twenty-second year in the classroom when Mother became ill and I took over her responsibilities in our home and supervised her care. This was a full time job so I retired from my teaching position during Mother's lengthy illness. She died two years later.

What would I do now? I began to pray for guidance in making a decision about how to spend the rest of my productive years. As always, God answered my prayer. A Christian colleague from the East coast called and invited me to contribute a chapter for a book he wanted to edit. The chapters were to be written by ordinary people who led extraordinary lives in spite of adversity and/or illness. How exciting to be offered an opportunity to give thanks for my blessings by writing a testimony of how God cares for me!

I submitted a chapter which focused on my professional preparation and life until retirement from my teaching position. Unfortunately, the inspiring chapters for the book were never united into a published manuscript.

I expanded my limited story to include information about my early years, my walk with God, my illness and my evolving ministries before I read about the Chosen Women movement. God had placed the present title in my mind, and I did not change it when the group's conference was scheduled in my city in 1998. If this work strengthens the movement, I will be grateful that God has used the story of my struggles for His purposes.

If you have not yet realized how God has guided you through your life, maybe my story will help you. Reading about my experiences may open the path to discovery of how much God has led you through your difficult times. I hope so!

My placement in schools where teachers encouraged me was no coincidence. How and why did I meet specific people who fed me with love and kindness at strategic times of my life? God was and continues to be my Guide.

To emphasize the power of God's Word in guiding and supporting me in affliction and trauma, I placed Scripture throughout this text. Because music influenced me during my developing years and plays a role now when I am adjusting to life changes, I inserted lyrics of secular songs and hymns in appropriate places.

The Psalm which best describes my attitude and gratitude is 92.4 (TLB):

"You have done so much for me,
O Lord,
No wonder I am glad!"

Read on and you'll understand why I feel this way.

Acknowledgments

Special thanks to all who have looked beyond my disability to discover my inner self.

In appreciation for my mentors at all levels of my education who believed I had promise,

for my past and present caregivers who have made my life joyful,

for my loved ones who encouraged me in my Christian walk and ministries,

for my loyal supporters Nancy (Gass) Campbell, who suggested that I share my life story with Inspiring Voices, and Carole James-Wenzel, Carol Rittori, Judie and Stephen Henry and Judy Adolph who edited parts of this manuscript,

for all who have met me along my way, students, colleagues, friends, pastors, doctors, therapists,

and for Melanie Dawn Silva, my caregiver and publishing assistant, who in 2012 helped me revise the first part of this book and produce the 2001-2012 section.

1930–2001

Beginning My Walk

The Preparation

"For we are God's workmanship,
created in Christ Jesus to do good works,
which God prepared in advance for us to do."
EPHESIANS 2.10 (NIV)

LOOKING BACK AT MY LIFE to discover how I became the person I am, was a painful and joyful emotional experience. When I reached sixty-five, I asked myself, "How was God shaping me to serve Him?" I felt as if I were trying to put together a puzzle of an impressionistic painting without a photograph of the finished product as a guide. I began to describe my childhood by digging up memories of family members, of houses where I had once lived, old neighborhoods, the many schools I had attended, friends, previous teachers, and good and bad experiences.

I haven't been able to remember much about my environment and people, other than the family, that were critical to my early development. For some reason, my brain has blotted out most events and experiences of my first years, maybe because my early life was full of sadness. Nevertheless, most of my later years were full of happy and positive happenings as one of God's chosen ones.

What has happened to me that makes me perceive myself to be one of God's chosen beings? Although my early years were troubled, I feel there was always a thread of hope and joy which kept me together as I journeyed on my unique path toward God and a Christian life.

I now think it was God who held me up and shaped me for His purposes during my trials and sufferings. I felt loved and supported, even during my chaotic teen years. I survived in a family that was not a Christian unit and would be described today as dysfunctional. I learned to focus on my blessings through hardships.

During my preparation, God has known my weaknesses and motivations that made me act as I did. Being an expert Potter, He chose and shaped me for a special ministry. I think I am finally focused on His work for me.

The Early Years

Now I can see how God guided me in my early years. Yet He allowed me to follow my willful ways.

I was a depression baby born to a struggling, lower-middle class family. Married young and not yoked in faith, Mother and Dad began their life together with many aspirations for improving their status. My sister, Mildred, was born nine months later in 1925.

Mother and Dad separated before I was born, but they were united again shortly afterwards. Their discord was evident throughout my early years. I became used to stormy and calm periods. Dad, a handsome, talented musician, was surrounded by admiring women. He was also tempted by the vices of the twenties and thirties. Unfortunately, he didn't like performing. Mother encouraged him to develop his talent for arranging music for big bands, but this job didn't pay well and he wanted to make big money.

Mother and Dad lost their modest home during the depression. They were determined to rise above this tragedy and recover their spirit of enthusiasm. Neither had finished high school, but they were both hard workers. Mother, beautiful, intelligent, and self-educated, had a kind and accepting nature. Her genuine commitment to raising a family was demonstrated by her actions. Her goal was to have a happy home. She learned how to do everything for our comfort. She made our clothes and upholstered old furniture to give it a new look. We always had a cheery place to live with plenty of well-rounded meals to eat. Her unconditional love held the family together. I believe Dad loved her, in his fashion.

I think Dad viewed Mother as a trophy, his conquest. She encouraged him and believed he could do anything he set out to accomplish. He told everyone that she had been "Miss Pittsburgh," an untruth according to Mother. She thought he had related this story so often that he believed it.

Dad did not seem to accept his humble beginnings although he was always supportive of his parents and their strivings to improve their life. As an adolescent he played several instruments in an orchestra with his mother. He left high school to follow a musical career. When he was twenty, he met Mother in a dance hall where he was the featured banjo player for a big band. Mother said she fell in love with him when he played "The Song of India."

I think Dad's wish was to be better than he was. Unfortunately, he wanted to create his image as a professional person without expending the effort to get the education necessary to reach his aspirations.

Mother's wish to provide a stable refuge for the family was probably because of her insecure early life. She didn't want us to experience the sadness she felt as a child.

Mother's childhood was not the norm for the times. When she was two-years-old her father, a glassblower, became very ill and soon died of a brain tumor. Grandmother sent her oldest child, Fern, to live with a relative. Rather than separate her two youngest children, she placed them in a Christian orphanage. Mother spent the next eight years of her life in this institution. Grandmother visited the children as often as possible. She had little time because she held down two jobs to pay the remaining medical bills from my grandfather's illness.

At age ten Mother and her brother, Sheldon, two years older, left the orphanage to live with their mother again. Mother went to work after school each day in a butcher shop. She enrolled in business school after graduating from the eighth grade and later became secretary to the president of a big steel company at age fourteen. She was a bright girl.

During my childhood Mother didn't lose her interest in learning. She was always reading or studying something. She was so articulate on many subjects that people thought she was a teacher or a librarian.

I don't remember Mother talking about her childhood until I was older. She related later that chapel was the high point of her day at the orphanage. The hymns she learned in chapel helped her cope with the stress of institutional living and the problems she faced later in life.

Mother never sang these hymns in our home. But she was always humming or singing some tune. A song came to my mind when I was trying to recall the events of my early childhood that influenced my character. The song was linked with an experience that could have been tragic.

"Every star above, knows the one I love,
Sweet Sue, just you..."
(<u>Sweet Sue, Just You</u>. Harris & Young, 1928)

On Christmas Eve, 1933, I was standing on a chair next to the stove watching Mother cook candied sweet potatoes. She was preparing for the holiday dinner the next day. A typical three-year-old, I wanted to be in the midst of everything. Suddenly, I lost my balance and reached out for something to stabilize myself. I grabbed the pot of candied sweet potatoes. They poured over my face, covering all but my eyes.

As usual Mother had to cope alone with this family emergency because Dad worked nights. She gathered me in her arms, arranged for transportation and rushed me to our family doctor, who had an office in the basement of his house.

The doctor took off the top layer of potatoes, bandaged my face, and poured oil over the bandages. His instructions were to keep the bandages moist with oil. He also prescribed bed rest. With time and patience, he said, the oil would heal my wounds.

People often comment about how calm and patient I seem when others might be hysterical in trying situations. Sometimes they ask how I learned to be patient. I think my recuperation period from the burns was my first lesson in patience. I don't remember having been told how long I wore the bandages. I do remember that everyone around me talked positively about the outcome. Time passed slowly but hope was high while we waited for the day the bandages would be removed.

The waiting was a natural part of the recovery. I was learning that with time all things would work together for my good. Trauma was followed by calm. Later in life I found out that recovery would not always be the outcome of all illnesses and accidents.

I waited for Dad to sing my song, "Sweet Sue," on the radio every day during my recuperation from the burns. I was Sweet Sue. Chuck Shanks, my dad, Al, his brother, and their musical group, "The Shanks Brothers," played "live" every day on the local radio station, WSPD, in Toledo, Ohio.

My two eyes peered out of my face swathed in bandages as I waited for the hour. My song was the first one on the air. It was dedicated to the little girl listening at home for her father and uncle's voices to sing to her. I faced the wooden box, covered with cloth in the center (the radio), and thought my father's group was in it!

As I evaluate this period of my life, the constancy of Mother's loving care and her devotion stand out. God taught me that I could always count on my mother to be by my side in times of trouble. Dad expected her to carry the load in the home. Mother's stability made her a positive force in my life as a child and as an adult.

The bandages were never allowed to dry, and the doctor's prognosis was proven to be correct. The outcome of the recuperation was amazing. I did not have a single noticeable scar on my face. It was truly a miracle, and yet, because I did not know the God who performed it, I could not say *Thank You*!

After the burns, there were no visible scars.

The Pre-teen Tears

Favoritism, a negative development in any family, probably was accentuated by my period of recuperation from the burns. Who could be sung to every day and not feel special? I was a star, my father's favorite. Mildred, then eight, must have felt that I received more attention than she did, both from Dad and from

Mother who cared for me. I don't even remember her being part of the family constellation at that time.

Events in the Shanks family also led to a tight bonding between Dad's mother, whom we called Mom, and me. Shortly before the birth of my sister, Mildred, my Mom had lost her only daughter from a ruptured appendix and subsequent peritonitis. She did not live long because the year was 1925, and medical technology of that era could not save her. Dad and his parents wanted to name my sister Mildred after her deceased aunt who was perfect in everyone's eyes. To avoid dissension with her husband and in-laws, Mother, age seventeen, agreed. Years later Mother told me that she didn't realize the consequences of her having given in to the family's wishes.

Unfortunately, as time passed the two Mildreds' personalities did not turn out to be alike as the Shanks family unfairly expected them to be.

I was named Susan after my great-grandmother, Mom's mother. She lived with the Shanks family in Ohio while Dad, his sister and his brother were at an impressionable age. Her bitterness about the outcome of the Civil War and the loss of her family's plantation penetrated the household according to Mother. Living in Ohio surrounded by Yankees must have been difficult for her.

Great-grandmother Susan played the piano with music and by ear and added joy to the family with her playing. I don't know how it evolved into a family affair, but soon others were playing with her. Charlie, Dad, was her favorite probably because he was the most talented. Mother thought she supported him in his decision to leave high school before finishing so that he could pursue his career in the music business.

Great-grandmother Susan was alive when Mother married into the family. Mother and Dad lived with the senior Shanks for a time because these were difficult years. Work was hard to find because of the depression.

Great-grandmother Susan also paid more attention to Dad than his brother during his adult years. She felt he could do no wrong even when he was obviously not making the most of himself.

I don't know if Great-grandmother Susan was alive when my sister Mildred was born, but she died before I entered the picture. After my birth Mom showed little interest in Mildred and showered me with attention. I think I took my deceased aunt's place in her heart.

Our relationship grew because of our love of music, especially piano. Mom could play any song by ear. Whenever possible, after my burns had healed, she played and I sang and danced by the hour. I became very self-centered and proud of my supposed talent.

Now I realize that my character formation, linked to over-attentive family members, Dad and Mom, had its negative aspects. I wanted my own way and knew who would grant my wishes, if possible. When crossed, I often cried to manipulate the family. What a challenge I was to God who was trying to mold me into a giving, not receiving, person.

The attention might also have had positive effects. I think it helped me develop more self-confidence than I might have had due to my stormy family life.

I knew I was loved. I think Mother and Dad perceived me to be a special, unique creature. I was so sure of myself at times that I was capable of telling others, even adults, what I thought they should do, especially Dad and his brother who were always at odds about something.

Many holidays, when the brothers were not speaking, I told them how unfair it was to the rest of us to suffer from their refusal to gather as a family. Surprisingly, they listened, or I thought they did, because we did celebrate together.

My behavior did not always create a comfortable situation, but Mother was tolerant of my bossy ways. She never accepted my self-centeredness, but seemed to understand how these less than acceptable behaviors developed. I don't remember what she did to offset my undesirable conduct. I do know she never criticized me or Mildred nor made me feel unworthy of her or anyone else's love.

My first memory of having a sister was when I was five. We moved to Cleveland where Dad and his orchestra had a job in a large hotel. Mother, Mildred and I often went to the movies at night, and we walked through a graveyard, the shortest way home. They took turns pulling me in the wagon. One time Mildred tried to make me believe that the dead people would rise up and follow us home. I wasn't afraid because Mother didn't seem concerned. Mildred liked to tease me, but I wasn't sure when she was telling the truth or when she made something up. As I recall Mother wasn't critical of her behavior. She knew Mildred was only having fun and meant no harm.

After a year or so we moved back to Toledo and Dad and Uncle Al left the music field and opened a club that served meals and had a floor show featuring small dramas. Unfortunately, alcohol was the money maker for the "Club Oasis" and a problem for Dad.

Now both of our parents worked at night at the club. Mother was the cashier. Mildred was responsible for me at night and often during the day while our parents slept. I remember that she complained about this chore because I was not as cooperative as she wished.

Our parents still did not communicate effectively. Although I never seemed to be the topic of their arguments, I think Mildred was. I don't know what she did to aggravate Dad, but I recall Mother telling her that "talking back" to him only made matters worse.

The years flew by with little diversion. We shared few family vacations. Mother took Mildred and me to Pennsylvania to visit her family every fall before school started and every spring after school was out for the summer. We looked forward to these trips because the cousins were similar in age, and they were fun to be with. My maternal grandmother and all of her children lived in and around Pittsburgh, PA. The family described her as a "dyed-in-the-wool (very strict) Baptist," but while we were there she seldom went to church.

Every summer Mother, Mildred and I took a day trip by boat that traveled from Toledo to Cedar Point. We spent time at the amusement park and ate lunch on the boat, which had a dance floor on one of its levels. I liked to watch people dance to a real band. What fun!

One summer when I was about eight, Mother, Dad, Mom, Pop, Mildred and I squeezed into our car to drive to Kentucky to visit Mom's brother and his family. He and his sons were farmers whose houses were all on the same road. I felt as if I had traveled backwards in time when we arrived at our destination. Their house was a one-story wooden unpainted structure that was raised about twenty feet above the ground and supported by thick wooden stilts to avoid damage during frequent flooding of a nearby river.

Of course, there was no running water or inside plumbing. One trip to the privy (out-house) was too much for me. I refused to enter the smelly place. During our short stay, Dad drove me to the nearest gas station once a day when I had to go to the bathroom or I used a chamber pot. Other than that inconvenience I enjoyed the simple life of these relatives.

The sons and their families celebrated our visit every evening either by bringing delicious southern dishes in for dinner or by taking us to their church for a sing-along. Talk centered around hunting and fishing, universal topics for men. When we left, we were grateful for the fellowship we enjoyed, but mostly for the conveniences that awaited us at home.

Our lives changed drastically when we moved to a house nearer the restaurant. My memories of Mildred became more vivid during our years there. She was very independent and capable.

Mother had a thyroid operation soon after we moved. I think Mildred had to assume too many responsibilities during Mother's recuperation because she complained that she was doing what Mother should have done. Most mothers didn't work then. At the time I thought the remark was typical of a teenager and didn't pay much attention to her. Now I wonder if her words and tone of voice were a symbol of a deep resentment toward Mother that would later erupt into a storm between them.

This was the period when we rented our biggest bedroom to two men from New York who sang at the club. I don't remember where the rest of us slept when they were in our home, but they were so nice to have around they didn't seem like strangers.

Like most performers of that time they were tired of hotel life. They traveled from city to city most of the year and had little time to be with their families.

Occasionally, Mother invited these renters to join the family for a home cooked meal. In return they prepared dinner for us. They added harmony to our home. It would have been horrible to share our space with people who didn't respect our privacy. But they were kind men who sang as they washed their socks in the basement and played golf during their free hours. Even though they were very talented, they lived a nomadic existence. Observation of their life style cured me of my desire to have a singing or dancing career in show business.

The pressures of trying to make money, the temptations of drinking, and the general nature of night club ownership did not contribute to a stable family life.

When Mildred and I stayed Saturday night at our uncle's house, we attended Sunday school with my younger cousin, Sheryl, and her baby sitter. The Shanks did not go to church as a family. After being up all Saturday night until the crack of dawn, our parents never mentioned Sunday morning worship as a possibility. Sunday was a day to catch up on lost sleep.

Regular church involvement did not seem important to me either until I was in the fifth grade. Then, a friend invited me to a downtown church where I was later baptized and became a choir member. This was my first experience with group singing. My friend's family became my Sunday family.

With this family's support I had taken my first step toward becoming a Christian. Many more were needed for me to develop Christian behavior. My roots were still on very shallow ground. I was beginning to understand that the dimensions of Christ's love are beyond measure. Fortunately for me, the Lord is patient with His children. He led me and grew me in faith according to His plan.

> *"I will instruct you (says the Lord)*
> *and guide you*
> *along the best pathway for your life;*
> *I will advise you*
> *and watch your progress."*
> **PSALM 32.8** (TLB)

Singing in the church choir increased my interest in music. I took piano lessons and learned to read music. I spent a lot of time with Mom and Pop (Dad's father). My favorite pastime was still dancing and singing as Mom played the piano.

We children took part in seasonal sports, swimming, ice skating, biking, and sledding, at nearby parks. We designed clothes for paper dolls, created villages with houses made with playing cards on the rug in the living room, and played board games, Chinese Checkers and Monopoly, by the hour. I read, read and read! After school I performed plays with two sisters who lived around the corner from our house.

We wrote and acted them out in our attic, not unlike the Louisa Mae Alcott family.

My time in fifth grade was joyful because of my work on the school newspaper. One of a few students with a typewriter at home, I became a reporter for the school. We produced news that was interesting to the children and the teachers.

At home Mother and Dad's evident problems diminished the joy I felt when in school. The situation was impossible to ignore. Their discussions, although held in private, were heard easily. I often listened to them from my adjoining bedroom or from where I sat eavesdropping on the top steps of the stairs next to the living room.

To cope with my sadness, I began writing poetry and letters that were addressed to, but never sent to, my unhappy parents.

The club closed and Uncle Al was drafted into the army. Dad decided to open another club, bigger than the first, by himself. He must have had someone backing him, but I never knew who his partners were. I felt Mother did not approve of what was happening.

Years later I heard the club, which was on the Michigan/Ohio border, was involved in gambling. This illegal activity was ignored by the sheriff, Dad's friend.

The end of the fifth grade terminated with tearful good-byes. Mother and Dad separated and without any discussion of my wishes, I was moved to my paternal grandparents' house. At ten-years-old I needed to be sheltered from the family storm. Dad called their home his residence although he was seldom there.

Mother and Mildred went to live elsewhere. I visited them occasionally but didn't feel comfortable in the home where they rented a room.

Dad took me to the club Sunday evenings for "Family Night," which featured dinner, dancing to "live" music and a floor show. Watching the families interact made me aware of how different ours was. Parents, children and grandparents enjoyed their dinner, danced and laughed until the show began.

I sat at a table with my Dad who often had to excuse himself to attend to business. Rather than eat alone I began spending my time backstage watching the female performers apply their makeup. This experience solidified my previous negative feelings about entering show business. The heavy makeup they wore made the beautiful girls look artificial and, at times, grotesque.

When I entered sixth grade at the new school, all but one of my new friends had united families. The children had lived in the same houses and had attended the same school since kindergarten. I began to realize that not having a mother or father was a rarity. Divorce was not common in those days and widows and widowers with children remarried quickly. My life style was typical of the '90s, not the '40s.

The new school didn't have a newspaper or any other extra-curricular activities to develop our social skills. My teacher seemed concerned about me. She chose me to be her mathematics tutor. The most handsome boy in the class needed tutoring. I began my work with gusto!

Junior High in Michigan

I finally began to fit into the new class when the club closed and Mother and Dad reconciled. We moved to Adrian, Michigan, a small town near Toledo, where I attended junior high. Dad worked as a public relations coordinator in the factory of a high school friend.

In Adrian, housing was a problem because during this war time many people had moved there for wartime work. We rented a small converted upstairs apartment in an old home. We were very crowded. There was a lot of turmoil in the family, and I couldn't understand how Mother and Dad thought we could live together.

Dad made many promises to Mother, but they were soon broken. I found myself forced to take sides during their arguments. I was unhappy most of the time. My sulking and pouting behaviors probably didn't help the situation at all.

Teachers always seemed to understand my situation. I don't know how. The Michigan teachers were no exception. I never talked with one about my family or the other schools I had attended. They probably noted many schools on my record. By the eighth grade I had gone to four different schools. Even when my parents were together, we moved a lot. Maybe there were notations in my file about the different people responsible for me through the years. God knows.

"I once had a gown, it was almost new,
oh the daintiest thing, it was sweet Alice blue;
with little forget-me-nots placed here and there,
when I had it on I walked on the air..."
(ALICE BLUE GOWN, McCARTHY & TIERNEY, 1919)

The teachers at the junior high were kind. I was chosen to sing "Alice Blue Gown" at the mother-daughter tea. My voice, not the best, was improving. My years of living in a musical family taught me how to sell a song.

Only two girls in the Michigan town befriended me. Other girls, including my neighbor one year ahead of me in school, treated me coldly. Years later, another younger neighbor explained why. During the summer the local girls often temporarily lost their boyfriends. The boys were attracted to the Ohio beauties who spent their summers at a nearby lake. Because I had moved there from Ohio, the girls viewed me as the competition, a boyfriend snatcher.

The Adolescent Years

Because I lacked friends I did not rebel when, after the eighth grade, Mother and Dad told me they wanted me to change schools. Mother had talked Dad into sending me to a local boarding school, St. Joseph's Academy, where I could receive an excellent college preparatory education. The Adrian high school was not accredited, and someone suggested it might be easier to be admitted into a university if I graduated from an accredited school. Nobody in our family had gone to college. At home we had never even discussed the possibility of me going, but teachers seemed to expect a college education to be my goal.

Another reason for choosing a new setting for my education was my behavior. Mother thought I needed discipline. She was having trouble managing me because of Dad's tendency to indulge me in my every desire.

Harmony was still absent in our home. The year before Mildred had graduated from high school, and she went to live in Toledo again. Mother tried to interest her in enrolling in Sienna Heights, the university associated with St. Joe's, but Mildred did not want to continue in school. She moved back to Toledo to work and live independently.

The boarding school, run by Catholic sisters, was an extreme contrast to my free life style. My three roommates were friendly, and we bonded into a harmonious group quickly. Dad, who was a 32nd Degree Mason and Shriner, requested that I be excused from religious services. His wish was granted except for Sundays when I was to attend Mass. I settled in physically, but was to remain unsettled emotionally throughout the year.

I do not know how Mother and Dad paid for this year away from home. Mother was working in the office of a small factory, and Dad's position probably paid a modest salary. I suspect that his employer and friend, who donated generously to the school, helped sponsor me in some way.

In spite of the emotional support of my roommates and the excellent study habits I was developing, I was miserable. I couldn't wear lipstick. I couldn't whistle. No boys attended the school. We had our mail inspected. We wore ugly, smelly wool uniforms. I couldn't wait for the school year to end, and I was determined not to return when the school year was over. I wanted out!

Dad was proud that I now wore hats and gloves and acted like an elegant, poised young lady. I think that he viewed me as another of his trophies.

At St. Joe's I began organizing parties for the dorm. The nuns were quick to praise my accomplishments, especially in music. My roommate and I sang "Whispering Hope" like angels according to our singing teacher.

"Soft as the voice of an angel,..."
(**WHISPERING HOPE**, HAWTHORNE, 1972)

I was releasing my frustrations during my singing and piano lessons and practice. But I was no angel. I broke all the rules. I chewed gum, whistled, cut my hair without permission, talked during silent periods, etc. I always looked horrible because my punishment was running the dishwasher after meals. The steam straightened my hair out. I pouted because I considered the schools "prohibitions" unreasonable and said so to anyone who would listen.

Talking after hours led to a sleepless night I'll never forget. When President Roosevelt died, the nuns called everyone into chapel for a special prayer hour. They knew President Truman was a Shriner and thought he would ruin our country.

My three roommates and I discussed the situation when we returned to our room. Of course, this was after hours. The discussion turned into a heated argument, and we didn't realize our voices were getting progressively louder until suddenly the door opened and there stood the nun who slept in an adjoining room with beds for eight elementary school girls. She was a large woman who seldom smiled.

She ordered us out of the room and into the hallway where we stood in our night gowns paralyzed with fear. She led us to a stairway across from her area and told us to sit on the stairs, ten steps apart, and think about the punishment we should receive the next day. The window at the top of the stairs was open and a cold breeze was turning us into icicles when one girl quietly returned to the room for her blanket. As the night progressed, one by one we went to bed. Not the girl on the top step. She was determined that the nun would see her there the next morning when she went to chapel and lighten her punishment. What happened? At five in the morning, the sister left her room, head bent down. She never saw my roommate perched on the top step.

We never spoke of this experience to anyone. As you might guess, the night on the steps was our punishment. Because we were all healthy, none of us caught a cold or suffered from our lack of sleep. But we were all convinced that we didn't have enough self-control to live in this world of silence any longer. Would our internment never end?

The Mother Superior called me in to talk about the way I was behaving. She told me my face would begin to be permanently wrinkled if I didn't stop frowning and pouting. She said I had a beautiful smile and should share it with others. I never forgot this warning. For the rest of my life I tried to smile in all circumstances, even if I was crying inside.

Besides this good advice, I left St. Joseph's with two other gifts: improved social skills developed by living and sharing with three cooperative girls my age and excellent study habits that served me well during high school and the eight years I was climbing the educational ladder.

*"In my troubles I pled with God
to help me and he did!"*
PSALM 120.1 (TLB)

After many tears and much pleading, my wish to go to high school in Toledo by commuting daily by bus was granted. I left the boarding school as did several of my new friends from Toledo.

Commuting was not to be the answer to my desire to attend the Toledo high school of my choice. The year began smoothly enough. Some weekends I stayed in town with my new friends and/or at Mom and Pop's to attend dances and parties. (They had sold their house and moved into a small mobile home. There was no longer a place for me to sleep.) I joined the Beta Sorority and soon enlarged my circle of friends, male and female.

Then the ax fell. The bus schedule changed and the buses stopped running during the hours I needed to travel. I had to transfer back to the Michigan school.

The last day before the schedule changed, a friend asked me to come to her house to see the puppies her cocker spaniel had just delivered. She didn't know I would not be back on the following Monday. As we petted the dogs I explained my situation. She excused herself and returned in a few minutes to invite me to move in and be a member of her family. Her mother had agreed without even checking with my parents or her husband. I was astonished. It was a miracle!

"You are the God of miracles and wonders!"
PSALM 77.14 (TLB)

God remained in charge of my situation all the time. Mother and Dad paid for my room and board, and I had a regular baby-sitting job one night a week to earn spending money. Mother told me that my new foster family did not have to keep me if I was a disturbance to their life. I tried to make myself wanted which was not difficult to do. My new sister and I enjoyed each other's company and developed lasting friendships with our schoolmates. We attended sorority and fraternity dances, school functions and sports events. We often had groups of our friends in to dance and eat around our fireplace. I was a typical teen of the times with one exception. If I didn't study hard and get good grades, I would not be able to stay in the Toledo school.

The study habits I had acquired at St. Joseph's were helpful in meeting my goal to earn excellent grades at DeVilbiss. But now I had no teacher to plan my study schedule. I needed to discipline myself and stick to my designated homework time. As soon as I returned from school I went to my room to complete my assignments. Then I reviewed my class notes for the approaching tests. My goal was to over-learn the material so that I could "ace" the examinations in all of my classes.

After completing my work, I joined my foster sister for play time. Inside we danced and sang. Outside we rode bikes, and occasionally played tennis when weather permitted. Winter days were short so we had little outside activity from December until April. My high grades demonstrated that this routine served me well.

Although we both lived in Toledo now, except for family gatherings at my aunt and uncle's, I didn't see Mildred. She announced her marriage during my junior year and asked me to be part of her simple wedding. I accepted with pleasure. It was the first time I was a bridesmaid.

Until graduation from high school I lived with my foster family except for vacations and summers when I returned to Adrian. I earned money while at home by cleaning the houses of our neighbor and her sister. I also received an allowance for completing various household chores and ironing Dad's many white cotton shirts. My summer savings paid for school clothing the following fall.

A few months during my senior year I left my foster home to stay in a rented room near the school with Mother. She had separated from Dad again. When they reconciled, as expected, I went home to live with my foster family.

My senior year was one of the most exciting and rewarding of my life up to this point. I bloomed into a productive member of the 1948 edition of the Pot O' Gold yearbook advertising staff. A group of us attended a press conference at Columbia University in New York. We took the subway to our destinations and played bridge at night in the girls' rooms. Our chaperones were very understanding and lenient because we were trustworthy.

During this last year I was chosen to collaborate with students from other city high schools to run a local radio station, WTDS. I became part of a three-some of girls, called the Gremlins, who performed at pep rallies and sports events.

The 1948 DeVilbiss Gremlins: Lou, Jeanie, and Susan with her hair up in knitting needles.

My greatest joy was being a member of the school's a cappella choir that sang at various business clubs during luncheons and at school and church functions. At the end of the year I planned the senior prom with congenial committee members.

I had previously participated in the school's annual talent show, the Deviltries, as a choir member. Now the production became my focus at the end of this last year of high school. I was chair of the theme committee and had a substantial singing role.

"Gonna take a sentimental journey,
Gonna put my heart at ease,
Gonna take a sentimental journey,
To renew old memories..."
(SENTIMENTAL JOURNEY, GREEN,
BROWN, & HOMER, 1956)

Besides singing in the choir in the Deviltries, I was chosen to harmonize "Sentimental Journey" with a friend who was my on-stage husband. In the musical, we were on our way to honeymoon in San Francisco. Frisco Frolics was the theme of the musical that culminated an eventful year.

"Sentimental Journey" was one of many favorites that we sang on hay rides, while washing dishes, and when traveling with the a cappella choir on the bus to off-campus concerts. The words of the song had no sentimental impact at the time. Now they symbolize what I am relating in this book.

Mother had surprising news that spring. She asked me to go to the doctor with her. He confirmed her suspicions that she would have a baby in the fall.

My reaction was positive. Maybe this child would bond Mother and Dad more closely. I hoped so. I had plans to enroll in Michigan State University. It was a short trip from Adrian so I could come home when Mother needed my help.

The year ended with a splash. My foster family hosted a pre-prom lawn party for our friends. My sister and I with our mothers made hundreds of dainty sandwiches the night before the party. Graduation was a joyful occasion, but was sad too. I had to leave my family that had cared for me so lovingly during, what were in many aspects, troublesome years emotionally.

The choir sang for the baccalaureate at the church. I was on the program for the school banquet. Fifty years later I was shocked to read in the school reunion booklet that scholastically I was among the top fourteen students in the graduating class of five hundred and two.

"To God be the glory -
great things He hath done..."
(To God be the Glory, Crosby & Doane, 1972)

As I look back I think singing in the choir was the stabilizing force in my life during high school. During those three busy high school years I had often gone to church with my foster family, but I had never felt comfortable in the youth group. I also attended church several times in Adrian but didn't like going alone.

There was a big void in my life. I didn't recognize God as the giver of all of my blessings. Yet He continued to love me through His grace and still guided me in spite of my indifference.

Picture taken at the end of my high school days.

The Freshman Experience

I moved back to Adrian after graduation. Because of Mother's pregnancy I assumed many of the household duties. In the fall I planned to enter Michigan State University as a freshman.

I drove to Toledo often during that summer to attend parties hosted by women's fraternities that had chapters at State. While there I sold Dishmasters, a kitchen aide made in Dad's workplace, to my friends and their neighbors. This money was for special needs beyond my Michigan State tuition that Mother and Dad paid.

I enrolled in the fall as a resident of the newest dorm, East Landon Hall. Several friends from high school also attended Michigan State and we participated in an exciting orientation.

My major was Education with special emphasis in Speech Correction. At that time few jobs were available for women in Mass Communication. For this reason preparation for a position in radio, my interest, was not practical. I wanted a career with promise and one that would provide me with an opportunity to help others.

My friends encouraged me to run for a class office with them. In the fall I was elected Secretary of the

Freshman Class. I became a member of Kappa Alpha Theta Fraternity the following January. As a Theta, I signed up to be a reader for blind students, our philanthropy. As a representative of East Landon Hall, I was also an active participant in campus life. These activities together took a great deal of time.

The first of my family to attend college, I felt, surprisingly, no pressure to be a super-achiever. I was pressed to stretch my meager budget to join the Thetas, and I did this primarily by making my own everyday clothing and sharing clothes with my friends. I was an independent, maturing student.

Mother gave birth to my brother, Bob, eighteen years my junior, on Friday, November 13th. I was home for the weekend waiting for the delivery. Afterwards Dad wanted to celebrate by eating at the local Elks Club. He told everyone we met about being a proud father of a handsome, baby boy. He ate and then drank until I knew he was unable to drive. I was embarrassed when he told everyone we met that I had come home from college to take care of him. I hoped that Dad's behavior was not an indication of how he would act in the future. Time would prove that it was!

Bob was named after Dad who nicknamed him "The King" because Prince Charles of England was born the next day on the 14th. During the course of his life he was called Bobby and Bob by family, Chuck by teen friends, and later, Charles.

From November on I came home from MSU many weekends to help Mother. I hopped rides with the Adrian fellows who were always returning to visit their parents or to see their girlfriends. Mother's blood pressure skyrocketed during Bob's delivery and remained high, but controlled with medication, the rest of her life. Dad's drinking also skyrocketed but was only controlled periodically.

Over the Christmas break I had a big argument with Mildred. The crowd in Toledo planned a big party for New Year's Eve and a friend asked me to be his date. Mother and Dad also had an invitation to a party and didn't want to leave Bob with a stranger. I called Mildred to ask if she and her husband would come to Adrian to babysit Bob. For some reason, I can't remember why, she didn't want to come.

Our parents had not asked for Mildred's help nor had she offered her assistance the whole year. They had given her many things for her house and that had created a problem between Mother and Dad. For some reason, Mother had a hard time persuading Dad to give Mildred anything. I think it was because of her "take and not give" attitude. Although I did not mention this situation, I did say I thought she should assume this one task. She agreed, but with hesitation. We had never really been close before then, but after this incident our relationship was strained.

After a successful year filled with many social activities, I began a summer of keeping house and caring for Bob. When Mother and Dad received an invitation to join some business associates for a vacation in Canada, I urged them to go. I was a responsible well-trained baby sitter. They were gone a week and on their return they seemed eager to be back home. I had enjoyed taking care of Bob, playing house with a real baby was fun.

To repay me for my summer work at home Mother and Dad insisted that I deserved a holiday before I went back to State. They arranged a trip to Los Angeles so that I could rest in the home of musician friends and see the sights. It was great to go to jazz sessions and concerts in the Hollywood Bowl. But I was tired and would rather have stayed home. Shortly after my return I became ill.

Walking with Jesus

The Turning Point

ON THE NIGHT OF AUGUST 14, 1949, a month after my nineteenth birthday, the ambulance arrived at our house quickly. The doctor had diagnosed my case. I didn't have the flu as we thought. My high temperature, pain and weakness were from a virus. The diagnosis was POLIO.

What is polio? Why did I fall in the bathroom? Why were they in such a hurry to get me to Ann Arbor? These questions ran through my mind as my family made arrangements for someone to come in to care for my brother who was now nine-months-old. I was being rushed to the emergency room to the University of Michigan Hospital. Mother and Dad would follow in our car.

A spinal tap confirmed the doctor's suspicions. Not only had I contracted polio, but both spinal and bulbar types. I was quickly moved to the contagion unit in the children's ward. An iron lung, a cylinder on legs big enough for a person to lie down in, was in the room awaiting my occupancy. I had entered a new era of my life.

Enjoying an ice cream cone at Devil's Lake, Michigan, the weekend before contracting polio. My nickname was "Bare Shanks" because I dressed according to the lake style, a bathing suit covered by a man's shirt.

I was too sick to ask, "Why me?" I just wanted to know how soon I could get out of the lung. When would I stop hurting? The fever from the polio virus went through my body like a tornado. It destroyed many motor terminals in the spinal cord that had made movement possible. I could only move my head and the toes on one foot. My facial muscles were not paralyzed, and I could swallow liquids and solids. Fortunately, my sensory nerves were also unaffected so I had bowel and bladder control.

Soon I knew I would never care for myself nor walk alone again. I didn't know then that I would be carried through life by God, His angels, and His servants on earth.

Was I prepared for the many adjustments and challenges ahead of me? God knew and I would know in time. In His time, His plan for His chosen one, ME, would be carried out.

A New Life

"For I know the plans I have for you,"
declares the Lord,
"...plans to give you hope and a future."
JEREMIAH 29.11 (NIV)

After years of having been more independent than most children, I began my new life as a dependent person. I was uncertain of my future in a land of the unknown.

"...tho' tossed about
With many a conflict,
many a doubt,
Fightings and fears within, without,
O Lamb of God, I come! I come!"
(JUST AS I AM, ELLIOTT & BRADBURY, 1972)

I had not been affiliated with a church since the fifth grade. But the words of "Just As I Am" came back to me quickly as I sang it while lying on a stretcher in the Hospital Chapel. It became a stimulus for tears of release and my first call to God for help. 1949 was the year I began to use a wheelchair for my journey through life as a post-polio quadriplegic and a Christian. I prayed for salvation and asked Jesus to direct my life in the path my Heavenly Father wanted me to follow.

The contagion period elapsed. I had undergone water therapy and stretching to diminish my pain. Then I began to ask questions. How did I get polio? Nobody knew.

What is polio? I learned that polio, a contagious disease of the central nervous system, is caused by a virus. In 1949 there was no vaccine to protect people against the virus.

I was not the only person in our town to be a victim of the epidemic. Our paper boy and several other children also contracted it. Fear was high in our home. Mother and Dad came to see me in the contagion unit of the hospital, but they were careful and followed instructions to protect themselves and Bob from the virus.

Years later, doctors discovered the virus which causes this paralyzing disorder. They think the virus enters the system through the mouth or nose and attacks the nerves that control muscles. The early symptoms, fever and headache, can be mistaken for the flu as mine were. I didn't vomit, as most patients do. I didn't have a stiff neck or back until the second day of my illness.

Polio is also known as poliomyelitis and infantile paralysis. The paralysis is usually noted within a week during the contagious period.

Bulbar involvement in polio causes breathing problems. A variety of artificial respiration methods have been utilized with polio patients through the years. The iron lung was used at the Hospital when I was admitted. My body was first enclosed in the "tank" and then my head was thrust through a hole in the end of it. The hole was bordered by a rubber collar which was tightened like a purse string around my neck. When the side door to the lung was closed and the neck opening tightened, all outside air was cut off from my body. I felt as if someone were strangling me. My anxiety changed the rhythm of my already deficient breathing. I was not in synchrony with the lung's forced breathing pattern. My body was not only extremely uncomfortable in the tank, but I was terrified by what this "monster" was doing to me.

The nurses wanted me out of the iron lung as much as I needed to be released from its grasp. The extent of my paralysis made it very difficult for them to care for my personal needs through the narrow opening in the side of the lung. As soon as my fever lowered I was moved to a regular hospital bed and introduced to a chest respirator. After several days, the nurses began taking the respirator off for an increasing number of hours during the day.

People today have seldom seen an iron lung or a chest respirator unless they have visited the Smithsonian Institute in Washington D.C. These antiquated breathing machines have been replaced by more comfortable devices.

"...those who hope in the Lord
will renew their strength.
They will soar on wings
like eagles; ..."
Isaiah 40.31 (NIV)

The nurses and the rehabilitation team at the Hospital had a positive impact on my initial adjustment to my new body. My night nurse knew that I had the capacity to sleep without the chest respirator. She conspired with Mother and Dad to force me to depend upon my own muscles for night breathing. I was afraid I would stop breathing if I went to sleep. She told me that nobody would come to visit me until I tried to sleep without the respirator. At the time she seemed like a witch to me. But she became angelic when, after the first trial night, I reached my goal. I held God's outstretched hand all through that night.

"...for the Lord upholds him with his hand."
Psalm 37.24 (NIV)

I also leaned on the Lord for strength after I was released from the contagion unit and was allowed to have visitors. I was often drained emotionally after my friends left from trying to think of how to put them at ease when they came to see me.

My most draining visit was in mid-September when my Michigan State boyfriend, a forestry major, came to the hospital. I don't remember how he found out about my illness. Maybe Mother answered his letter to me from the forestry camp he was attending. She knew I was eagerly awaiting his return. He made a date for our encounter. I was anxious for him to come because I had decided to break up our relationship.

You may wonder why I made this decision without talking with him about the future. Maybe I was being idealistic or a romantic but I saw myself as a block in the road to his dreams.

We began dating at the beginning of the spring quarter. I had seen this handsome young man twice, at fall and at winter registration. Our last names, both beginning with S, placed us in the same registration group. He was my ideal physically. He just needed a white horse to be my Prince Charming.

When I saw him in the spring quarter line, I was chatting with a girl who lived in my dorm. I told her of my attraction to him, and she said she knew him and would introduce us. I was so excited that I couldn't say much, a rarity for me. He must have had a similar reaction to me, because he said little but asked if he could call me. Was I walking in the clouds? You bet I was!

Our dates were mostly on campus. We walked through the woods surrounding the complex of buildings, canoed on the river, went to his fraternity parties and mine, and enjoyed swimming in a nearby lake. He knew the name of every tree and wild flower. I, who only knew that a Christmas tree was a pine or fir, was amazed at his knowledge. I was learning to appreciate nature for the first time. We never talked about God or our beliefs, but he must have been as awed by His creation as I was. Our time together was peaceful. I could communicate with this gentle man.

With these memories in mind and his goal to work among the wonders of nature, I made the decision that I would share with him during our approaching visit. I had practiced what I was going to say as if I were preparing for a part in a play. When he entered my room, he looked pale even under his sun-tanned skin. His sister, whom I had never met, came with him. She seemed to be holding him up as if he were about to faint. I guess my weight loss of almost thirty pounds was a shock to him. And of course I was in bed because I was not strong enough to sit in a wheelchair yet.

I told him I was glad to see him and that I thought it would be best if he did not visit me again. I knew that with my condition I would not be able to live an active life as I had before. My days in the woods with him were wonderful memories I would treasure. I wished him well and said I hoped we could always be friends.

All through this "speech" I felt like another person delivering a message with little emotion. Inside I was hurting, but no one could tell because of my exterior calmness.

The impact of my message was evident. He seemed stunned, but did not try to convince me to change my mind. He and his sister left quickly. I did not see him again until two years later when I spent a weekend at the Theta house in East Lansing. Someone had told him I was coming and he stopped in to say hello.

A Theta sister who knew him told me later that he married after graduation and went to work in a management position for a large department store in his home town. Had his wife refused to live with him in the wilderness? When he visited me at the hospital, I thought I had done the right thing to discontinue our relationship. Now I'm not so sure I did.

"I weep with grief;
my heart is heavy with sorrow;"
PSALM 119.28 (TLB)

After this visit the tears I was holding back burst into a storm. The emotional catharsis cleared my head of unrealistic dreams. Then I began adjusting to my loss in my usual way--I got busy! My focus was on rehabilitating the few hand and arm muscles that were beginning to move at my will. I was unattached and ready to begin building myself up.

"Never forget your promises to me...
they give me strength in all my troubles;
how they refresh and revive me!"
Psalm 119.49-50 (TLB)

My therapy was scheduled in the morning, and afternoons were for resting. Two Michigan students, a high school friend and the boyfriend of my Michigan State roommate, visited me about every other evening. He cut my hair and she did my nails. We laughed a lot at his antics. I felt like my old self when with them, but I needed to widen my social horizons. God had placed the perfect person in my life to help me in this area, my a.m. nurse who became my main advocate.

This lovely woman, who was very wise, recognized my needs immediately. She found a wheelchair that had been cut down to fit an elderly lady she had cared for. The family was willing to sell it to us. It fit perfectly!

Previously I had been forced to sit in a huge chair that was five or six sizes too large for my childlike body. There were no chairs made for children then. I felt as if I could sit in this chair without falling. (In 2012 I am still using the chair at home.)

My advocate encouraged me to maintain my college appearance and interests. She would not prepare me for bed before the end of the day shift, as was the custom in the polio ward. She insisted that the 3-11 p.m. nurses dress me in my sleeping attire late during their shift after my college visitors left. I was not to be considered sick.

This nurse also planned activities in the Hospital to help me accept my changed status. As often as she dared, she took me into the employee's restricted dining room for socialization with abled young people. The patients on my ward were either children or married. None shared my interests.

My advocate also invited all of the handsome male interns and residents to my room to talk with me. She fed them the food brought by visitors who viewed my weight loss, from 115 to 85 pounds, as a post-polio problem. My right hand was beginning to move so she kept me busy writing thank you notes, which looked like a first-grader's, to my gift givers.

Because my father had played in an orchestra for the Annual March of Dimes Ball in Adrian for several years, the Crippled Children's Society was generous in supporting my treatment. Dad arranged for the physical therapists to work with me on weekends to speed up my recovery process.

My regular physical therapist, who became my life-long friend, was an inspiration. Legally blind, his fingers could distinguish lack of blood flow and consequential discoloring of the extremities by feel. He kept up my spirits and was influential in planning for my continued rehabilitation.

I needed encouragement after a resident-in-training who gave me my first muscle test made me realize the severity of my quadriplegia (paralysis of all four extremities, neck, and trunk). The doctor, who came to my room alone, graded each muscle verbally as zero or trace until I interrupted him to ask if I could improve. He announced flatly with a sardonic smile that I would hardly be skiing next year. I suddenly realized that I would probably never walk again and that I was fortunate to still be alive.

This upset was the first, and, fortunately, the last of my negative rehabilitation experiences. Nurses, physical therapists, and doctors continued to be very supportive. Two friends, U. of M. students, brought me books to read and talked about my return to college. My parents visited me as often as possible.

The doctor's muscle testing made me face reality. Years later another Christian asked me whether I had ever prayed for a miracle cure. I hadn't. I prayed for improvement and for the will of God to be done. My faith was either not strong enough to expect a cure or I was super-realistic, I don't know which. But I was grateful for any small movement that I could make.

> "... Thou art the Potter;
> I am the clay.
> Mold me and make me
> after Thy will,
> While I am waiting,
> yielded and still."
> (HAVE THINE OWN WAY, LORD.
> POLLARD & STEBBINS, 1972)

Looking back on how the Lord timed my next moves and molded my future convinces me that He sent special people to direct me. Their example was significant in my growth toward becoming a better person than I might have been without polio. John, my blind PT, was one of those special folks. On New Year's Eve he arrived at the Hospital with a box for a bottle of Four Roses. Inside were four roses (flowers instead of whiskey) to celebrate my acceptance at the Foundation in Warm Springs, Georgia (WS). We would fly there in two weeks.

Susan and John (PT) looking forward to their trip to the Warm Springs Foundation.

During the dismissal talk with my parents, the head of the Bone and Joint Department (now called orthopedics) told them that I could live a good life in excellent health. My world had not ended.

My adventure at WS was another positive step toward my acceptance of a new life style in a wheelchair. I was flown in an army stretcher airplane, with the help of the March of Dimes, to WS for ten months of intensive treatment for my zero and trace muscles.

My physical therapist was allowed to fly with me on the army plane, but my parents had to take a commercial flight. Our plane had an unexpected layover in Minnesota where we waited eight hours at sub-zero temperatures for passengers from a nearby army base. Mother and Dad arrived in Atlanta and became frantic after five hours when the controller couldn't find a record of our flight. Were we lost in space? No, but I was flying high because for the first time since I contracted polio I was able to feed myself on the plane!

Near midnight we landed in Atlanta safe and tired. I was taken by ambulance to the Foundation. At 2 a.m. they placed me in the ward for female teens, probably because I was transferred from the children's ward at the Michigan Hospital.

When I awoke the girls showered me with questions. Had I ever danced? Did I have a boyfriend? They were hungry for information about girls in the *outside* world. Many had been at the Foundation for operations on their growing bodies that kept them bed bound for years. I was grateful that at 19, my growth was completed and I didn't have to walk through adolescence in their shoes.

The Foundation was built by President Franklin D. Roosevelt and persons who donated to the March of Dimes. The staff was dedicated to the rehabilitation of polio "victims." The President had gone there to exercise in the warm water when he was recovering from polio. He saw the benefit of having polio specialists trained in one location of the country. With this goal in mind he began inviting outstanding people to join him in planning and building the Foundation.

Roosevelt had died before I went to Warm Springs, but the lively environment he developed and the positive team approach to therapy he encouraged lived on.

Warm Springs offered patients a full schedule of therapy and water treatment planned by their rehabilitation team. After thorough muscle testing, a rehabilitation team of specialists compiled the findings to formulate a unique therapy plan for each person. Patients beginning therapy for the first time spent the first weeks of their stay in the brace shops. I lay on a stretcher for hours while the brace and corset makers fitted and refitted me for full-length leg braces and a long line corset. Between these sessions I was lifted into the pool for water therapy. The warm water felt wonderful. The muscles of my legs moved slightly in the water. I wanted to stay in the pool as long as possible.

On land, on the other hand, I was dead weight. I could not turn over in any direction when placed on the floor mat. My physical therapist and her assistant stood me up every day. They locked the knee guards of my braces and lifted me into a standing position between parallel bars. The therapist pushed my feet forward one at a time to move me to the other end of the bars. I held on to the bars as well as I could. It was torture for all three of us.

Mother and Bob, now eighteen-months-old, came to Georgia later in the spring and lived for several months in a small house in the town of Warm Springs. They came to the Foundation every afternoon or evening to visit me. Dad drove down occasionally. According to Mother, Bob was very hyperactive when Dad was around. Dad's drinking had increased, and he insisted that Mother and Bob return to Michigan. When they left, I became more active in the social life of the Foundation, but I missed their visits.

In late summer I was in for a surprise. The four young men who had provided my transportation between Adrian and East Lansing the previous year arrived in Georgia to visit me. They were driving Mother's car! I don't know how the trip came about, but evidently they had been calling to inquire about my progress. One lamented the fact that their cars were not good enough to make the long trip to Georgia to see me. In character, Mother offered the use of her car and even paid the extra insurance needed to cover them during the trip. She was grateful for the help they had been with my commute the previous year and knew I would be happy to be with them again. We had a wonderful time during the few days they were in Georgia. The photographs they sent me afterwards of the Smoky Mountains were like a guided tour through that beautiful country.

A few months later the doctors began talking about the time when I would also go home. My periodic muscle tests showed that I was not getting any stronger. Activities of daily living (ADL) became our focus. My therapists and I began practicing transfer methods that a small person like Mother could use to move me. The nurses and therapists teamed up to prepare me for life without twenty-four hour care.

In October I was dismissed from the Foundation. I had learned to sleep all night in one position, and I could be slid on to the bathroom stool with help. Two people could move me in and out of my chair to the car with a sliding board. Mother could assist me into bed alone with the board. These were the keys to the nearly normal life I have led for over sixty years.

Everyone who had the good fortune to receive treatment at Warm Springs benefited physically and emotionally. Our family of patients and therapists gave us courage to enter the outside world. We learned to face architectural barriers without panicking and to ask for and receive help gracefully. And most importantly, I learned to accept my new self and the unexpected.

When they were notified about my dismissal, Mother and Dad had to make some decisions quickly. I could no longer live in our two story house, and there was no physical therapy available in our Michigan town. Dad was now traveling during the week in his new employ for a Detroit company. Mother and Dad decided it was best to build a one-story ranch house near Detroit, in Toledo. Mildred and her family, Mom and Pop, and my aunt and uncle lived there.

Although Dad had vowed never to buy another house after the depression, now there did not seem to be a choice. We couldn't find a rental house I could use without making many modifications which would be costly. Dad began working with a builder and soon found a lot in Toledo for our new one-story home.

"...for you are my fortress,
my refuge in times of trouble."
PSALM 59.16 (NIV)

Our barrier-free house was not completed when I was dismissed from the Foundation. What could we do? My *foster family*, still our dear friends, took me into their home again and cared for me. There were no bedrooms or a bath on the first floor in their house either. They converted their dining room into my bedroom and a portable toilet was set up in the kitchen which became my bathroom. My foster sister took care of me most of the time. This was when I began to realize that when one door closed, God would open another one for me.

I began physical therapy at a local clinic and started to be evaluated periodically by a doctor in Chicago, Illinois. Several months later I again left my foster home. Mother, Dad, Bob and I now called our house on Talwood Lane home. Therapy was available nearby at the Crippled Children's Hospital. As soon as we were settled in our house, I began therapy in the pool at the Hospital.

Accepting Reality

"... At the end of the storm is a golden sky
And the sweet silver song of a lark.
Walk on through the wind, walk on through the
rain, 'Tho' your dreams be tossed and blown.
Walk on, walk on, with hope in your heart,
And you'll never walk alone."
(YOU'LL NEVER WALK ALONE,
HAMMERSTEIN II & ROGERS, 1968)

One day I sat at my piano in our new home and picked out the notes of this Rogers and Hammerstein song with two fingers of my right hand. The tears flowed. I felt so alone. But I wasn't. God knew who to put in my path to carry out His plan for me. The lyrics of this song often come to my mind as I face challenges. For this reason I included some of the words in the title of this manuscript.

Settled in the town where I had attended high school, I began to think of the future. Not of normality, but of how I could cope with my condition and develop skills to contribute to my care.

After several months, I returned to Warm Springs to undergo a muscle transplant to give me a useful right thumb. The surgeon split the extensor muscle of my right wrist. He threaded a part of the muscle around to the palm of my hand, attached it there, and extended the muscle by adding a tendon taken from my left leg to it. The tendon was then threaded through the area where the muscle that moves the thumb to the index finger is attached (opponens muscle). A button was placed on the outside of the incision to make sure the muscle/tendon would remain in place. It was a work of art that is very difficult because the muscles of the hand are delicate and integrated into a complex whole. The result was successful. I could now grasp to pick up objects and push my chair slowly in the house.

My pool treatments were the highlight of my week. I was exalted by the freedom of movement I felt in the water. The buoyancy was hypnotic. Then I had an accident.

That day the physical therapist stood me on the side of the pool where I could hold on to a bar. The water was breast high. She turned to talk with another therapist when my hands slipped off of the bar and my legs buckled. I was under the water before I could utter a sound.

A great feeling of peace and silence traveled through me. I was drowning. I don't know how long I was submerged. But when I regained consciousness, the therapist and several others were holding me over the raised edge of the pool pounding my back. I sputtered and coughed up water until I could breathe freely.

After this experience I had second thoughts about my goals. I knew God had work for me to do or I would have drowned. It was not time for me to die. I had to get on with my life and find out what that work was. I was not gaining strength in my present therapy. I decided to focus my energy on getting stronger and continuing my education. I couldn't spend my life in a swimming pool! I had to prepare myself for a career.

My Toledo Theta friends encouraged me to seek counsel about my future from the State Department of Vocational Rehabilitation. Unfortunately, the counselor would not support me in the program I wanted to enter, teacher education. I was considered too paralyzed for a teaching job. But I was given funds to attend classes in accounting at the University of Toledo (TU). At this point my mother and I began our team efforts to prepare me to support myself.

The Toledo campus was as ideal for a person in a wheelchair as one could find in those days. It was built on a hill. The first floor of the main building was facing a busy street and was on the street level. The lower level had parking nearby and was kept free of snow and ice during the winter months.

No architectural barriers restricted me at the University. We entered the building through a service passageway that led to a hand operated freight elevator that could take us to all of the floors. If the freight odor was too strong, we could get off at the first floor and use the automatic elevator to move from one upper floor to another.

Most of my classes were on the first and second floor. The central hallway was separated in several sections by heavy doors. One led to a tunnel constructed so that you could enter the library without going outside. In the 1950's wheelchair accessibility was not an issue, but I think the campus would have passed the Americans with Disabilities Act of 1990 (ADA) requirements. This legislation and other federal regulations relating to disability are described in the Encyclopedia of Disability and Rehabilitation (A.E. Dell Orto and R.P. Marinelli (Eds.), New York: Simon & Schuster Macmillan, 1995, pgs. 47-54). I never entered any of the bathrooms there so I'm not sure if I would have been able to use their facilities.

The first day of classes Mother took me and stayed until I was sure of getting to the next classroom. My plan was to ask the professor for permission to request help from the students. I explained my need and asked if someone would push me to my next class. Several hands went up, and I picked one girl who had attended DeVilbiss with my cousin, Sheryl. She became one of my good friends and best push-girls while I was at the University.

I sat in the hallway near my next class and studied when my classes were close together and went to the library when I had a break between them for several hours. Soon I found it hard to study there because the students in my classes were very friendly and wanted to join me and talk. Many were Sheryl's contemporaries and wanted to be my friend too. They always asked about how things were working out for her at Ohio State in Columbus.

The relationships I built with the students showed me that I could make new friends easily. My disability was not handicapping me socially.

I was adjusting, but Dad seemed unable to accept the stigma of my disability. He expected me to get better. I remember the doctor telling him that I was not a machine that would always work if plugged in right, but a person with a physically damaged system. My muscles might not be strengthened with exercise.

I could not regenerate nerves and improve beyond the limitations polio had imposed upon me.

Dad's drinking increased after we moved to Toledo. He was opposed to any discipline of Bob. A typical weekend was spent watching violent TV while Dad drank into the late hours of the night. Mother objected when Dad insisted that Bob be allowed to stay up with him. Bob became very absorbed in the emotion of the atmosphere and did not go to sleep long after he went to bed. Mother and I prayed for a solution to this problem. It was time for a change.

Dad's behavior became more and more unpredictable. He was verbally abusive, but never harmed Mother or me physically. At my request Mother placed a noisy chair that was on wheels in front of my bedroom door at night. I wanted a warning if Dad wandered into my room. But fortunately, he never did.

Our family support system disintegrated with the increase in Dad's drinking. Mom and Pop were concerned about his behavior. Mom came to help with my home exercises and stretching almost every day. She always asked me what had happened the night before or over the weekend. When I related the events, she became angry and refused to believe me. Finally, I realized I couldn't continue with these confrontations. They were destroying our close relationship. I told her that if she didn't want to hear the truth, she shouldn't ask me because I would not pretend that we lived harmoniously under such stress. She still came to help us, but not as often. She relied on Dad for information, I guess, because she didn't ask me any more questions.

My aunt and uncle, who owned a small neighborhood club, were busy in their own world. They thought we should concentrate on Dad's success in his work and his increased ability to provide for our material needs and ignore his drinking.

During this time Mildred filed for divorce. With her two small children, she had her own problems to solve. She had to build a support system for her little family because we were not able to help her much.

United in our struggle for survival, Mother and I bonded more closely. We began to pray for ways to cope and keep calm in chaos.

We spent little time talking about the upsetting events of the day. Neither of us had ever prayed aloud, but we each began to talk to God in our own unique way.

With a large four bedroom house, a four-year-old and my care, Mother always had plenty to do. She kept busy, and I learned that activity also helped me through trying times. When things were really rough, both of us kept *occupied*. I cleaned everything I could reach over and over again.

Dad's uncontrollable and unreasonable behavior led to the breakup of our family in 1951. When I see the anxious faces of frightened women and children shown on TV, the past begins to haunt me. The policemen who are called in to handle domestic abuse can offer little help. I empathize with these families because I walked that road with Mother.

In spite of my home situation I had a fairly normal social life during the next two years and experienced romance three times. I had known one of the young men in high school. One was a classmate at TU. The third was a medical student from Maryland whom I met when visiting a Warm Springs roommate. I had seen enough marriages break up at Warm Springs to know that it took a special type of person to make a marriage between a disabled woman and an able bodied man work. The three relationships did not last.

My boyfriend from high school was looking for someone to make decisions for him. I had been the planner of most of our dates when I went with him before. Now I was different. I wanted a more dominant partner.

My Toledo University friend was a special person, but he was from a Jewish home. How could two people yoke who had such different religious beliefs? I couldn't continue in a romantic relationship with him. He and his wife, a beautiful Jewish woman, have been my close friends throughout our adult lives.

The medical student was the oldest child of a happy Catholic family that didn't believe in divorce. He did not understand the problems we faced daily. He thought I should accept Dad's abuse of alcohol and associated behaviors regardless of their consequences.

I prayed for a happy life with, or without marriage. Many of the abled single women I knew were unhappy because they were single. They were always looking for Mr. Right. I have had many wonderful male friends, but marriage did not seem to be in God's plan for me. I never felt nudged to search for a mate.

"Day by day, and with each passing moment,
Strength I find to meet my trials here.
Trusting in my Father's wise bestowment,
I've no cause for worry or for fear."
(DAY BY DAY, SANDELL-BERG & AHNFELT, 1972)

Mother and I began attending church where I had gone as a child. We prayed for strength and guidance. After many discussions with our pastor, Mother attempted, with success, to arrange a friendly separation through a lawyer who was Dad's friend. Mother was granted money to build a modest home that was accessible for the wheelchair. A small amount of alimony and child support for Bob paid for food and expenses.

Dad faulted the church and me for the breakup of the family. He said if he had his way I would be put in an institution. Even though I had never asked for his support, he told me the church would have to pay for my schooling if I were to continue at the University. He wouldn't. But I knew my Heavenly Father would always support me. If I were to graduate with a career, we would find the means to finance my education. I wondered many years later if Dad remembered his *threat*. God had provided for our needs.

This was the first and last time I was the target of Dad's verbal abuse. The change in Dad's attitude toward me was difficult to understand. He had always been kind to me. Then I think I found an explanation for his behavior.

Dad stayed in the ranch house with us until our new home was finished. His hostility did not decrease and soon I thought I knew why. During moving preparations I began looking through old magazines in his room before disposing of them. I found an envelope containing five hundred dollars in cash and a letter. He had either hidden it and forgotten where it was or thought we had it.

The letter from a beautiful New York pianist (a picture was enclosed) was a negative reply to Dad's marriage proposal made while he was still married to Mother. Maybe Dad thought Mother planned to use the letter to increase her settlement. He should have known that was not her style. She gave it to their lawyer and kept the money to pay for a fence for the new house so that Bob could have a dog.

> *"Help me, Lord, to keep my mouth shut and my lips sealed."*
> PSALM 141.3 (TLB)

I remembered the tenseness in our home years before when Mildred was a teenager. She often argued to get her way; she "talked back" to Dad. I tried to avoid verbal confrontations with him. I did not say anything to disturb the silence we endured while waiting for the house to be built. The outspoken member of the family was unable to talk without fearing reprisal.

What a relief when the divorce was finalized and we moved into our refuge! Mother and I began a concerted effort not only to survive on a very small budget, but to live a peaceful life. Each evening after dinner we sat around the table while I read from a book we thought Bob would enjoy. We all became engrossed in the "Little House on the Prairie" series and other books about families and animals.

Mother also read to Bob every night before he went to sleep. Their favorites were "Winnie the Pooh" and children's Bible stories. I could hear the happy sounds of the laughter from Bob's upstairs bedroom. It was music to my ears.

Right before the first Christmas we lived in our new house, Mildred asked Mother to take care of her two small children while she was recuperating from gall bladder surgery. Mother tried to convince her to postpone the operation until after the holiday. At forty-five, Mother had more than she could do. Bob was five and my condition hadn't changed. Mildred was furious and refused to talk with her doctor about waiting. Although she was divorced from the children's father, her mother-in-law, who no longer had any of her family at home, cared for the children. Mildred didn't speak to us for ages after that. I cannot recall how long we were estranged from her, but finally we began getting together again.

Some people might have considered our routine in the new house boring, but we were happy surrounded by a supportive church family and loving neighbors and friends. In 1998 a young matron, who had lived near us as a child, wrote me the following after Mother's death. "Especially when faced with adversity I stop and think of all the trials and tribulations she faced head on with grace. It gives me strength to carry on." Mother's example went beyond our family.

Dad's visiting privileges included weekends and holidays. Bob spent most of his time with Dad at Mom's mobile home. (Pop had died several years before.) When Dad moved to California, Bob wanted to live with Dad there, but Mother said not until he was old enough to care for himself. He was always sent home early from Dad's before his visit was to end as a punishment for something or other. Dad had told Bob not to mind Mother. Now the tables had turned, and he would not mind Dad either. Bob's attitude made things difficult in our home. He began to resent limits Mother imposed, and he could not maintain a harmonic relationship with Dad.

I had no desire to communicate with Dad during this period, and he never entered the house when he picked Bob up. I sat by and watched. Mother and I did not talk about the past nor anything disagreeable that was happening. We knew that we couldn't change Dad and that rehashing the past would be bad for all of us, especially Bob.

Our focus was on the positive. We needed to prepare me for an independent life. I would need to manage my affairs when I was alone in the future. Whatever decision I made, as long as it was well thought out, Mother found a way to work toward my goals. My grades in accounting at the University were excellent, but I did not like working with numbers. I was still attending physical therapy without making any noticeable improvement.

Now Bob needed tutoring in reading. His teacher felt he should go to someone outside the family for help. But we were pressed financially. We were referred to a lovely retired teacher who helped him at a reasonable rate.

My friends convinced me that I had found the answer to my search for another area of training to work with people. I should return to school to become a reading tutor. The rehabilitation counselor agreed to support me in this endeavor because it was something I could do at home.

Preparing for a Career

After extensive physical therapy, five years post-illness I still had very little muscle return. My doctor suggested that I begin to work exclusively on my head. He recommended that I resume my studies full time and cut down on therapy sessions. He warned me against pressure sores and advised me to change my position for at least ten minutes every four to six hours. (For over fifty years I have followed his advice and have as yet never suffered from skin breakdown.) I was blessed by sensation in my body, bowel and bladder control and excellent health. As predicted by my physician at the University of Michigan Hospital, I began to live a full life.

> *"When I pray, you answer me, and encourage me by giving me the strength I need."*
> **PSALM 138.3** (TLB)

The Rehabilitation stipend covered the costs of several classes, but it was not enough for full time tuition. Even though the University of Toledo was five minutes from our new home, we lived in Lucas County, not within the city limits. A municipal university at the time, tuition was high for county residents. Many students commuted to Bowling Green State, twenty-five miles away, where the tuition was reasonable.

My Theta friends sent me to people they knew at the University to inquire about grants and scholarships to augment my stipend. All doors opened, and I began the Education program with great enthusiasm.

At the end of my first year of study a third grade teacher in our neighborhood school offered to train me to tutor using her method. With the backing of my professors, I quickly became a reading tutor.

My social life while in school consisted mainly of attending young people's groups in church basements. As soon as the eligible men found out I was not looking for a husband, we became friends. They picked me up, *literally,* for activities. We had a mixed musical group that met to sing in our home regularly. I also sang with two other friends with disabilities. Occasionally, the trio and mixed chorus performed for special events in nursing homes. It was fun because everyone was relaxed and ready to laugh at the slightest mistake.

Mother and friends who transported me to school during the next three years never complained about riding in smelly freight elevators and using the University's tunnels to avoid snow and rain. I finally reached my goal, a Bachelor of Elementary

Education and the promise of referrals from teachers in our neighborhood school.

But my professors had a different plan for me. Several felt I should enroll in student teaching and demonstrate that I could handle a classroom of students. The chair of the Department of Education had many reservations about my being in a classroom every day, and she tried to stop me from enrolling in student teaching. My professors insisted that I be given an opportunity to fail.

I hired a student push-boy and we walked two blocks, even through rain and snow, to school each day. At the end of the term my supervisors gave me excellent evaluations. They even wanted me to return to teach in the school the next year. But that was not to be.

A group of administrators from the Toledo Board of Education was invited to an International Dinner that my students had arranged with my guidance. The principal told the group that the school needed me the following year to cover a vacant position. I was not acceptable to the administrators!

Their suggestion was to place me in the school for the handicapped. The children enrolled there needed much physical assistance. One of my disabled singing partners was teaching at that school. She couldn't handle the children physically, even though she had almost normal use of her arms and was ambulatory with crutches. How they expected someone in a wheelchair with little use of her extremities to help these students was beyond me.

> *"We are ... perplexed, but not in despair;..."*
> 2 Corinthians 4.8 (NIV)

The principal, angered by this unfair judgment, was determined that I should be given a chance to teach. Unknown to me, she negotiated with the priests from the adjoining parochial school. They agreed to hire me as a teacher of a small class of seventh graders. I also taught English to the eighth graders. These children had never been taught as a unit but had always been a large combined class.

Again I found a student, a sixth grader, whose job was to push me three blocks to school through wind, rain, and snow. I felt like the Pied Piper each morning and afternoon as we were followed by a large group of children we picked up or left off along the way.

Before beginning this *real* job, I began to think about my initial educational plans. If I could tutor reading and other subjects, why couldn't I help people with speech problems in my home? My rehabilitation counselor thought that a private practice in speech was an acceptable idea. The State of Ohio granted me one more year of tuition to study speech and hearing. The Kappa Alpha Theta Foundation awarded me a five hundred dollar scholarship that would defray my expenses. Without economic restraints I enrolled in summer classes at Bowling Green State University. I was convinced that helping people with communicative disorders was the job for me.

The campus was not entirely accessible, but the speech and hearing clinic, faculty offices and the classrooms were housed in one large "U" shaped single-level building. The psychology classes I had to negotiate were in temporary buildings with one step at the entrance. During the summer, faculty offering my other classes in the education department moved our meeting place to the first floor of an air conditioned building without elevators for the comfort of everyone. I was accommodated without any stressful encounters with anyone.

Fulfilling a Dream

After teaching in the fall and spring and studying another summer at Bowling Green, the professors encouraged me to begin a master's program. They offered me a job working as a lab assistant in the speech clinic ten hours a week at one hundred dollars a month the next fall. The promise of spring semester housing on the campus during the winter months was my reason for enrolling full-time in the program. The registrar gave me phone numbers of commuters who lived in Toledo. I soon contacted the ten people who would provide my transportation for the fall semester.

"We can make our plans,
but the final outcome is in God's hands."
PROVERBS 16.1 (TLB)

But there was one obstacle that sabotaged my spring housing plan. Late that fall there was a big fire in a school dorm in Chicago. Because of this tragedy the Housing Department retracted the offer to let me live in a campus dorm. I thought I could not continue to commute each day through the terrible winter. But all of my chauffeurs rallied to assure me that regardless of the snow and ice they would see that I got to school. Mother was willing to drive me if anyone were ill. I knew that this was a sign that I was to complete my degree.

What a marathon! Every day I faced the elements with as much of a smile as I could muster. Some days I left at seven o'clock in the morning and returned home at ten at night. A fellow student assisted me with my personal needs during the day. If I lived through *this* period of my life, I could do most anything through God who strengthened me! (Philippians 4.13)

After finishing my M.A. program my major advisor and mentor recommended that I look for a job as a speech therapist. He also suggested that I think about getting a doctorate in the future. I was surprised he thought someone would hire me to work in a clinic. I couldn't believe my ears. But I listened.

We were also to receive another message from God to direct our future. Mother and I met a lady in the drugstore who began a conversation with us about the nasty Ohio winters. She had multiple sclerosis and spent her winters in Arizona. She asked why we didn't go there. We had never seen this person before nor since. Was she an angel talking to us about the Promised Land? How could we leave family and friends and go without a job?

Analyzing our way of life in Ohio left little doubt that this was not the best place for us to live. When it snowed I left my mark everywhere I went. What was it? A big puddle where I sat to thaw. Ten years of struggling through ice and snow in the wheelchair were enough to make us begin to consider the move.

Stabilizing My Walk

Our Desert Years

AFTER GRADUATING FROM BOWLING GREEN, Mother and I drove to Phoenix to look for work. At the time there was only one clinical facility, Gomper's Clinic, which offered speech therapy services. But many of the small school districts in Phoenix were beginning to hire therapists. My experiences at Toledo University and with the representatives of the Toledo Board of Education prepared me for the administrators I met in Phoenix. 1960 was *not* the year of equal opportunity employment.

During two interviews I was told that there would soon be positions in outlying school districts. I could substitute teach in grade and high schools until a speech therapy job became available. I would qualify for a clear credential if I took two additional classes. I was encouraged.

We returned to Toledo and put our house up for sale. By the time I took the two needed classes, the house was sold. We were leaving the snow and setting off for an adventure that would shape the rest of our lives.

In March Mother, Bob and I went to Phoenix by car. When we arrived, the Arizona sun was a tonic for all of us after the frigid Ohio winter. We found an apartment that was convenient for the wheelchair. It had a large swimming pool and catered to families.

The family that owned the units welcomed us. The owner's wife had multiple sclerosis and also used a wheelchair. Her cousin lived in one of the units so that she could care for her and help with household tasks. The men in the family offered to lift me into the pool if I would like to get in the water on the weekend. Recalling my last pool experience I accepted on condition that I could wear a life jacket. Although the jacket made me a clumsy bundle to handle, they understood that I needed the protection. The struggle with my "Mae West" was worth it. I enjoyed this treat while we lived there.

I began substituting in Phoenix elementary schools shortly after we unpacked. When the schools closed for the summer, I rested. My last years at Bowling Green had sapped my energy. All was quiet on the home front because Bob was spending more time with Dad who now lived nearby in Los Angeles.

Winters in Ohio were very cold, but the summer heat in Phoenix was almost as unbearable. I applied for a job as speech therapist at Gomper's and began to substitute in elementary schools. In October, the day that my sixth grade substitute position could have become my permanent job, Mother came to the school at noon with exciting news. The administrator of Gomper's had called me for an interview. They, too, had a place for me. I accepted the position at Gomper's with eagerness.

During my two years at Gomper's, I learned that many graduates in speech and hearing had not received the excellent training that I had at Bowling Green.

The American-Speech-Hearing Association decided to change our name from therapist, which meant we needed a referral from a physician, to pathologist. Professionals trained in treating people with communication problems were now known as speech pathologists. The new name reflected our independent diagnostic and therapeutic role on the heath care team.

My mentor at Bowling Green had recommended that I work toward a doctorate. Should I enroll in an advanced program? I could teach others to do what I was doing to help people, and they would learn how to offer better services as a result of my additional training. I began to consider where and when I could go. First I had to find a way to pay our expenses while I was a full-time student.

My social life in Arizona again revolved around the Theta Club and church activities. Mother and I participated in the initial rush for the new Theta chapter at Arizona State. Our family of friends ranged in age from young children to senior citizens. It was difficult to think about leaving Arizona, but there were no graduate programs in the state.

Mother and I planned a tour of the West to talk with the faculty at universities that offered a curriculum in speech pathology. We started by visiting Bob who was spending his vacation with Dad in Los Angeles.

I saw clearly through an unpleasant experience that Dad was trying to live vicariously through his children. Again I was the star. While we were all seated in the living room, Dad began calling people.

One sounded like a potential employer. He said his daughter in a wheelchair, who was a speech pathologist in Phoenix, was in town. According to Dad I was traveling through the West looking for schools that offered a doctorate in my subject. Stanford was my first stop after leaving L.A. He made it sound as though he were supporting me. At one point I told him that I had come to visit and wished he wouldn't make any more calls about me. When he didn't stop, his wife reprimanded him and said I had reason to dislike what he was doing.

Later, when thinking about the scene, I felt sorry for Dad as he seemed to be groping for positive points for himself through my achievements and strivings. This, I believe, had been a behavior pattern throughout his adult years. Unfortunately, Bob, then fourteen, was not applying himself in school and Dad could not brag about his grades or accomplishments. Dad was obviously disappointed in him and showed it.

Bob and Susan in Los Angeles

The drive to Palo Alto where Stanford is located was easy and scenic. When we arrived I called for an appointment. Most faculty were on vacation because classes were not in session. I was scheduled to talk with a professor who taught in the department but not in my area of speech pathology. He said the staff would not support me for grants nor scholarships for doctoral study. My two years of satisfactory clinical work were ignored. The reason given was their inability to place a particular disabled student who had graduated from their program. (I later met this M.A. graduate at a state convention in California and heard about her successful private practice.)

Other schools we visited didn't offer the doctorate. We returned to Phoenix discouraged and with no future direction. Or so we thought.

Following His Lead

My supervisor at Gomper's knew of the situation at Stanford. She suggested that I contact the chair at Louisiana State University, her alma mater. She remembered students in wheelchairs on campus. But that was a few years before. Surely by now the campus had become more accessible. I decided to make inquiries immediately.

Correspondence with the Admission's Office was encouraging. The summer tuition was right ($50 for nine units) and dorm housing was available for families. According to the person who wrote to me the dorm did not have steps and the dining hall was also accessible.

> *"Since the Lord is directing our steps,*
> *why try to understand everything*
> *that happens along the way."*
> **Proverbs 20.24** (TLB)

When we arrived for the summer program, we found the dorm doors were flush to the ground. Surprise! Inside was a flight of steps to the bedrooms that was more than Mother and Bob could negotiate. The housing coordinator who answered my letter of inquiry had never opened the outside doors of the dorm to inspect the bedrooms.

This turned out to be a blessing for us. We settled into a duplex close to the campus where we met two supportive families. The two front steps were ramped and the beds were new. Everything else was much in need of soap and water. As usual Mother did all of the necessary work to make the place into a cozy home. She could not control the humidity, but we did have a large window fan. We ran it continuously day and night when the heat became intolerable. Mother and Bob spent a lot of time visiting in the air-conditioned homes of our new friends, the owner's children, while I studied at the library.

The chair of the Speech Department welcomed me cheerfully with something like, "Well, young lady, how do you get around in that chair?" His attitude demonstrated to me that this was a place where I could grow with my limitations. He counseled me to take courses from three different professors during the summer session. He concluded by stating that at the end of the summer the faculty would meet and decide what our next step might be. After I looked over the department and knew the professors, he added, we could talk about the future. Was this the spot God had in mind for me?

Regardless of the three steps at the entrance to the Music and Speech building, I *knew* this was a place where I could learn and grow in the Lord. Many male students were always at the entrance to the building. They would continue to carry me across that barrier each day. I was sure of their support. Elevators lifted me to all of the other floors in the building. The library was completely accessible. At the end of the nine week session, the faculty offered to help me obtain a grant or scholarship. The chairman advised me to return to Baton Rouge when I was prepared to take the reading tests in French and German. I had not studied either language. What a challenge!

Graduate Study

Before going back to Phoenix, I went to the Bookstore and purchased the texts the Graduate School recommended for learning to read research in a foreign language. Both the French and German books were small and well-illustrated with many examples. My goal was to translate an article in one hour, using a dictionary, with 70% accuracy.

Fortunately, I located a retired language professor immediately upon our return to Phoenix in August. I quickly began to send out applications for financial support. I told my employer that if I were granted a stipend, I would leave Gomper's the following summer.

Because I had studied Latin for one year in high school, my teacher suggested that French, which had a similar structure, would be the language to tackle first. I read the practice material in the books and wrote out the simple translations using my dictionary and following the instructions. I put any word I thought would be useful on a 3x5 card that I kept by my side at work and studied whenever I had a free minute or was waiting for a client who was late.

After much study of French at night and on Saturday, I was ready to begin German in April. My teacher told me that we would have to hurry because she was leaving Phoenix in May for the summer. I studied during my lunch hours and breaks and burned the midnight oil at night and over the weekend with good results.

Our family constellation changed when we went back to Baton Rouge. Bob, now fifteen, did not like Louisiana so he opted to live with Dad in California. The big move brought us face to face with another obstacle. What would we do if we moved all of our furniture to Louisiana and I didn't pass the general qualifying exams? With my government training stipend in hand, which included support for Mother, and God's blessing, Mother and I again packed up and moved.

LSU Adventure

"Commit your work to the Lord,
then it will succeed."
PROVERBS 16.3 (TLB)

While waiting for our furniture to arrive in Baton Rouge, we found a clean, air-conditioned, one bedroom apartment close to campus. Here we hosted many get-togethers for the friendly graduate students from our church. Our lively discussions gave each student an opportunity to forget the tensions of our respective graduate programs. We relaxed while talking about the problems in the world beyond the University.

Mother and I again joined the local Thetas in rushing lovely southern belles for a new chapter at the University. We enjoyed the friendship of our new neighbors and people we met the previous summer.

The general exams, administered in the fall, were relatively easy. My Ohio training proved to be worthy of graduate credit. In the spring the faculty told me that when I completed the language requirements we needed to move. My program would continue in the new branch at the associated Medical School in New Orleans. In the meantime we were to apply for an apartment in the new medical student housing unit that would be open in May.

The French exam given early in the fall was a snap. I finished in time to go over my paper and correct several of my obvious errors. My name appeared on the Graduate School PASS LIST that was posted several days later.

Then I signed up for the next administration of the German exam. I had heard that 85% of the graduate students who took the exam failed the first time. I met several people in the department who were on their third and fourth trials. Yet after the exam I could not believe that my name was not on the PASS LIST because the articles had seemed relatively easy.

I made an appointment with the German professor in charge of the examination process to go over my mistakes. He opened our meeting by asking me if I had gone to a private or public school. I was surprised by the question, forgot about my boarding school year, and answered "public." "What did that have to do with my performance?" I thought. He explained that graduate students didn't pass his exam unless they had graduated from a private school. The University was a state school and many poor students, like me, went there. How was a person with ideas like this given the responsibility for coordinating the test?

I explained that I came to see my exam and was under a time restriction. Would he please show me my papers?

There were very few red marks on them. When I asked him to explain the errors, he began by telling me I hadn't done too badly (70% was the passing grade). A few hours of tutoring would assure me of passing next time. He recommended a tutor, a German student, who would provide the service at a reasonable price. Money was tight. I wondered how we could add anything more to our budget. He said four or five hours should be plenty of time to prepare me for the task.

What a time the tutor had with me! He was five or six years younger than I was and very pedantic. This young man was the perfect stereotype of a European professor. He wore his glasses on the tip of his nose and had the shabbiest and most ill-fitting clothes seen on campus. But he was a generous soul. I contracted with him for ten hours of help. I figured if five would prepare me for the test, ten would allow me to pass it with a high grade. He seemed pleased with our agreement. He graded my work at our apartment and asked me to translate several other articles for him to work on at home. I was surely getting my money's worth.

If I challenged him during our sessions, he abruptly told me that he was the professor and that students don't question the professor. Of course, I disagreed, and that often led me to explain that I knew English as well as he knew German, and that my translation had to sound as if a native speaker had written them. He accepted this fact and we got back to business.

Mother sat in the kitchen and laughed at the comedy we acted out.

After he felt at ease with me, he confided that he had entered my life because of a cause. The coordinator of the German exam was making graduate students hate German, and my tutor thought that he should be removed from his position of power. He was going to take the test when I did. His work would earn him a letter stating that he was proficient in English translation. If I didn't pass the exam, he would fight for the right to see and grade my paper. I was supportive of his idea.

The Saturday after the exam, a group of graduate students met at our apartment to study. The PASS LIST was to be posted in the hall of the Graduate School that morning. I asked Mother if she would go to see if my Social Security number and initials were on the list while we were busy. She refused because she had plans and wanted to do something else. She thought Monday would be time enough to know the test results.

After the crowd left, the phone rang. A female voice I recognized as my colleague asked, "Is this SJS, SS# ….?" What a fun way to find out that my name was on the PASS LIST!

With the language requirements behind me, I was eager to begin studying at the Medical School in New Orleans. Two weeks before our moving date in May, I became concerned because the inspectors would not let us in the building to see the apartments. We would have to find another place to live if I couldn't use the facility. Two days before our furniture was to be picked up, we were allowed into the building. We couldn't believe that in this supposedly barrier-free housing unit I couldn't use *ANY* bathroom.

A fellow doctoral student spent one whole day taking us from one unsuitable apartment building in New Orleans to another. We finally found affordable housing in an old apartment hotel one block from the Medical School. We could cook simple meals in the utility kitchen, we were granted free parking, and the school was within walking distance. When it rained we could use the tunnel between Tulane Medical School, Charity Hospital and the LSU Medical School. The Lord had led us to a convenient spot we could afford. We also were surrounded by wonderful people who, like us, were temporarily housed in the hotel.

After completing my courses I began to look for a research project. Neurological disorders fascinated me. A professor in the department wanted to know more about voice qualities associated with supranuclear palsy, also known as pseudobulbar palsy. He had seen several patients with this problem in the Charity Hospital Clinic. I was excited when he asked me to research this disorder with him.

I began to read the literature on the disorder. Many of the articles were in French. I located several doctors in the hospital who were fluent in French to correct my translations. Another exciting challenge!

Unfortunately, the five patients my major professor saw in the clinic were the only ones to be found in New Orleans. I combed the files of every hospital in town and only these five met the criteria for my study. The professor on my committee who represented the Baton Rouge faculty would not accept a study of less than ten patients with the disease. I had to find a new topic fast.

After spending seven months reviewing the literature on the topic, I was very discouraged. If we hadn't had our furniture in New Orleans, I would have been tempted to leave and forget about finishing my degree. I'd be a member of the large group of people with an ABD (all but dissertation) who never complete the last requirement for the Ph.D.

My major professor suggested that we study the effects of changes of pitch and loudness and aging factors on the opening and closing of the larynx (vocal cords) during sound production. I could investigate these variables in normal women. These laryngeal movements had been researched among some patients with neurological disease at Northwestern University in Illinois and were to have been part of our pseudobulbar study.

My committee agreed that the prospectus for this project was acceptable. Finding women who met the physical requirements to be considered "normal" sounded like a difficult task, but it didn't turn out to be a problem. My goal was to locate and test groups of women ranging in age from 20-40, 40-60 and 60-80 who didn't smoke, drink alcohol, and were in good health.

Medical School students, staff and volunteers at Charity Hospital and local senior citizen groups cooperated with me and were eager subjects for my study. Mother even packed up my recording equipment and set up my "shop" in a convent for black nuns in the suburbs. A priest friend from Toledo made the appointment with this group for me. The women, who were all cooperative and gracious, ranged in color from light skin to coal black. The Mother Superior invited us to join the resident priest for lunch in an elegant dining room with a lace tablecloth and cloth napkins adorning the table. We were treated like royalty and the food was delicious.

The nuns' repetition of the syllable (ha) in which the larynx opens and closes was very fast. The test was much like their chanting in church. Many of them had practiced this type of vocalization for years. Because of their high scores, I could only use a few of the tapes from each age group.

When I had collected all of my taped samples, the faculty approved my request to bring the equipment I needed to analyze my data to the hotel. As a student I never wanted anything to do with machines. Wouldn't you know I'd end up with a bedroom of equipment to run for my study!

A recently widowed lady, who had moved into an apartment on our floor in the hotel the same day we arrived, became our friend immediately. Her son, who was the program manager for a New Orleans television station, had free tickets to many local events, even private Mardi Gras balls. Mother provided the transportation, and she and our new friend enjoyed the social life of New Orleans while I studied. With no carpets to obstruct me, I could lock the deadbolt on the apartment door. I felt perfectly safe alone with the switchboard operator available in case of an emergency.

A retired judge and his wife from Shreveport enlarged our circle of friends. They came to New Orleans so that he could provide services for their over-crowded courts. Although we all moved after that year, we kept in touch with these sincere friends for many years.

> *"When sorrows like sea bellows roll,*
> *Whatever my lot, Thou has taught me to say,*
> *'It is well, it is well with my soul.'"*
> **(IT IS WELL WITH MY SOUL.**
> **SPAFFORD & BLISS, 1972)**

During our stay in New Orleans Bob wanted to be with us again. Many times before, when Bob returned from living with Dad, he would be an emotional wreck for months. Not this time.

Mother talked with our priest friend from Toledo and explained the situation. He suggested that I ask for extended grant money for Bob. He had been my dependent for the previous four years. The money would cover tuition for him to go to a boarding school across the river. We could visit him there until I was finished with my graduate program. Bob refused. Mother told him he had no other alternative this time. Either he could go to the boarding school or live with

Dad in California until I finished my degree. She knew our location in downtown New Orleans was no place for an emotionally upset adolescent, and we were unable to move at that time. After many discussions over the telephone, Bob decided to stay with Dad rather than go to the boarding school.

A short time later, Dad, whom we thought was happily married for the third time, committed suicide. Ruth, his wife, called to say she was sending Bob to Mother although he had not been living in their home. She said he had moved out and was staying somewhere else, they weren't sure with whom. Bob had returned to Dad's apartment to pick something up on the day of the tragedy. He was the one who found Dad's body after he had shot himself.

According to the family Dad left a beautiful letter for Bob. He never shared its contents with us nor talked about the experience. We felt it was not appropriate for us to question him about this horrible incident. We knew he would need professional help to recover from the shock and began to consider the options that could meet all of our needs.

Mildred told us later that Dad's act of desperation had not been a shock to her. Mom had said that our uncle and aunt would take Bob if we wouldn't let him join us in New Orleans. Neither of them knew anything about her plan. Dad then told Mildred that he would kill himself if she refused to take Bob into her home. What a devastating experience for her! Dad had talked about suicide to manipulate Mother for years so I was not surprised that he finally carried out his threat.

My reaction to Dad's suicide was disbelief. How could he do such a thing to Bob? Was the act supposed to make Bob straighten up and live right, not as Dad had lived? Was suicide to be the teacher to erase the emotional damage Bob had suffered? Was the letter Dad left the map Bob should follow on his road to change? I knew that my questions would never be answered.

I thanked God that Dad was no longer miserable and that he could no longer hurt anyone. I was grateful for my early memories of his love and of his dedication to his work. I had lost my father years ago when we moved from Talwood Lane. Dad's actions in our home had taught me not to follow his path. My grieving did not last beyond the time we received the call and Bob arrived in New Orleans.

We quickly began to restructure our lives. Fortunately I had completed my formal coursework. I was finishing my research and was ready to write my dissertation. I tried to arrange for my care in New Orleans so that

I could work as a speech pathology aide at the New Orleans Veterans Administration Hospital associated with the Medical School. I wanted to stay there until I had terminated everything for my degree, but I couldn't find a caregiver and did not want to live in a rest home without a relative nearby. We knew we all had to leave New Orleans. I faced the challenges of completing my doctoral work during that year in Ohio.

My major professor promised that he would not let my dissertation remain on the bottom of his mountain of papers. I began sending chapters to him for the red pencil (his corrections).

We found a rental house in a suburb on the outskirts of Toledo, and Bob agreed to enroll in high school. He was unable to sleep at night without having horrible nightmares. Mother arranged for Bob's psychotherapy evaluation, and he began his sessions immediately. After a few weeks he dropped out of school and transferred to another school near Mom's mobile home where he knew some youngsters his age. Again he didn't stay in school, but he did continue his therapy. The psychologist predicted that Bob would never finish high school and sadly to say, he was right.

Mildred and her new husband tried to help us, but Bob did not want to spend time with them.

Her children, typical teens, were having their own difficulties adjusting to a new father figure.

While waiting for my chapters to be returned, I mailed post cards periodically to my professor. Each contained a reminder for him to look at my work whenever possible. We kept the post office busy shifting my work to and from Ohio and Louisiana until graduation. The chapters kept coming back in a respectable time period.

To support the three of us, I began substituting in a school system in a neighboring small town, a district not far from the one that closed its doors to me before. My experiences there in first to seventh grade classrooms would take another ten pages to relate. What a great diversion and way to keep the rent paid!

The family reunions and time spent with friends helped us through our stopover in Toledo, not a pleasant period of our lives. Bob wanted a car, but Mother would not sign for him. His behavior had changed and it was obvious that he was on drugs.

Mother would be liable for others in the car if they were hurt when with him. She couldn't take the chance. She bought him a reliable motorcycle (not the expensive one he wanted) and he spent his waking hours with his old friends or on the telephone at home. He constantly wanted to be given money but wouldn't do anything -- household chores or get a job -- to earn it. I expressed my anger when he kept yelling obscenities at Mother if she insisted that he help in some way. Mother was afraid that he might strike me when I spoke out about his verbal abuse, but he never hit either of us.

Learning that he couldn't bully us into giving him money, Bob left home. Because he was not eighteen, the psychologist told Mother to report him as missing. He stayed in Juvenile Hall until the court placed him in a friend's house as a foster child. When Bob was eighteen, after two years of trying to help him, we left Toledo. He was able to make his own decisions. He wanted to remain there, but we couldn't live in that climate.

Throughout these trials Alan, a lawyer friend, advised and encouraged us. He also reminded us of past problems that were resolved and said, "This too will pass." And it did.

My Ph.D. degree was granted and now I was qualified to teach at the university level. I had passed all exams and completed my research. At graduation, my dissertation chair, who supported me through some very trying times, told me he called me by a nickname when I wasn't around. Now it was time to tell me what it was. SMILEY!

*"Praise the Lord, O my soul,
and forget not all his benefits…"*
PSALM 103.2 (NIV)

From our previous years of battling the ice and snow, Mother and I knew we had to search for a university where the weather would allow me to move about freely during all seasons of the year. Again we began to pray for guidance. Where did the Lord want to plant us next?

Our Place in the Sun

*"But if by a still, small voice He calls to paths
that I do not know,
I'll answer, dear Lord,
with my hand in Thine,
'I'll go where You want me to go.'"*
**(I'LL GO WHERE YOU WANT ME TO GO.
BROWN & ROUNSEFELL, 1972)**

The search for an accessible university in a warm climate was not easy. But then we are not promised a rose garden, right? My first stop was a temporary job at a university in Missouri. This institution was completely accessible for wheelchair users. I would have liked to stay there if it hadn't been in such a cold climate. The chair knew I was interviewing for jobs, and she agreed to allow me to travel whenever necessary. The faculty found us a convenient apartment, and the snow plows kept us moving.

Mother and I flew to several states for interviews. This was a trying time for her because she was afraid to fly. One time when we had to prepare for a landing without lowering the wheels of the plane, she was terrified. This was coming home from a trip to a southern state. I had received a puzzling reply to my inquiry into their position announcement. The chair of the speech area said that I met all of the qualifications for the job except that they preferred a male!

In my answer I said I could not meet that requisite, but I didn't think it affected my teaching skill. I was invited for an on-site interview.

There were a dozen or more steps at the entrance to the edifice where Speech was housed. Another door opened onto the driveway behind the building that housed a convenient room used for group therapy. From there we were led through a maze in the furnace room before reaching a freight elevator that carried us to the main floor for the interview. What a mess!

After the interview we were taken by car to a hospital to meet a faculty member who was recuperating from an operation. In the evening the faculty wined and dined us in an elegant home. As we visited I asked how they thought I could manage to get around on a campus with so many steps, and in their building with such obstacles. An audiologist said they invited me because they just had to meet a candidate with courage enough to question the system. Discrimination against women (and maybe wheelchair users, too) was still strong in that state. It was no place for me in 1966. I graciously accepted their warm southern hospitality and said I would look forward to seeing them at the next national convention.

By the end of the semester in Missouri I was offered a job in Florida. I was asked to stay in Missouri and teach an additional summer session. What a consolation to know I had become skilled and was respected by other professionals.

"Man proposes, but God disposes."
PROVERBS 19.21 (TLB)

My next two workplaces, in Florida and in Texas, were not to be permanent. During my interview in Florida I was shown a new building, next to the library, where the department was to be housed. I was excited because I could buy an electric chair and become less dependent on others to push me from building to building. The position seemed perfect. But it wasn't. When I arrived in August the department chair told me that their plans had changed. They had decided to remodel a group of apartments on a busy highway across from the campus. The department would remain there for a few years until a new health facility could be constructed on campus.

I felt deceived. Why hadn't they told me about the change before I moved across the country to work in such a poor physical plant? Classes were held in one apartment, and faculty offices were in another. They raised the back sidewalk with a wooden platform to connect the units and enable me to move between the apartments. Wind and rain assaulted me as I moved from office to classroom. I tolerated the inconveniences one semester and began to look elsewhere for work. The chair of an associated department, housed on the main campus, offered me a position teaching anatomy and phonetics. Speech pathology students were required to take these courses. But I wanted to teach in my specialty areas, aphasia and voice disorders. So I began searching for a department that would offer these courses, that was hiring and that was on an accessible campus.

The Texas facility was housed on one floor, but the campus was not accessible either. I was offered the challenge of developing classes in my areas of training, but the faculty politics were unbelievable. I stayed two years, which seemed like ten. I could not grow professionally in such an emotional climate. A colleague from my training years later told me he recommended me for the position when he left the program to teach elsewhere. He thought I could make a positive difference in the situation there. I tried!

Colleagues told me not to be discouraged. They said college professors often teach at several schools before they find a place where they feel comfortable and can develop their areas of strength.

My next job did not seem like an ideal placement either. My initial interview in 1970 at Fresno State University, later renamed California State University, Fresno, was less than satisfactory. The chair of the department forgot I was coming. Nobody was at the airport to meet me and Sheryl, who traveled with me from San Francisco. How was that for an entrance visit?

But Fresno's climate, the campus, the terrain, the traffic flow, the curriculum, the possibility of advancement professionally and the proximity to Sheryl's home in San Francisco, all added up as positives. I was offered and accepted the position at

Fresno State. Here was the place I would teach for the next twenty-two-and-a-half years.

The Communicative Disorders Department moved from the Speech Arts building to the recently closed Laboratory School during the first month I was on campus. Sidewalks were added for entrance into the area and curbs were ramped. A work crew removed part of the wall in the waiting room restroom. That change allowed me to use the toilet.

In 1969 Section 504 of the Rehabilitation Act became the law of the land. Architectural barriers were to be removed to make public buildings accessible to wheelchair users. Government money was available for making any needed changes. The entrances to many of the buildings were flush to the ground or ramped, and they had elevators to the upper floors. Others were spotted for renovation. During my first year at State, the faculty of the Rehabilitation Counseling Program applied for and were granted funds to eliminate other campus barriers. Changes in entrances to major buildings and additional elevator accessibility made the campus ideal for wheelchairs.

All of the modifications motivated me to purchase a motorized wheelchair. By now I could push my chair slowly on hard surfaces, but I was unable to cross thresholds at the doors to leave or enter a building.

When I bought the motor wheelchair, Rick, the husband of one my students, was looking for a hobby. His work in an office was confining, and he enjoyed tinkering in his garage. He offered to service my chair annually and repair it when necessary. Because of his attention, my chair had very little down-time during the twenty years I used it on and off campus. Another blessing.

The new chair allowed me to move about the campus alone to attend and participate in university-wide meetings. It also earned me the nickname *Hot Wheels* among the students. The freedom from physical exertion when pushing my manual chair increased my energy level and gave me a feeling of independence I hadn't known for years. I began to contribute to community health planning committees at night. I was a new creation!

> *"...let your light shine before men,*
> *that they may see your good deeds*
> *and praise your Father in heaven."*
> **MATTHEW 5.16 (NIV)**

The excitement of a growing department, the confidence of having achieved a long-awaited and difficult goal, and the presence of family nearby made the next few years some of the best in my adult life. With the promise of tenure in 1973, after living in apartments since leaving Toledo, I put a small down payment on a condo, a haven for Mother and me.

Just before we moved, Mildred called to ask if she could come to live with us. Mike, her twenty-one-year-old son, had died suddenly from viral pneumonia the year before. He had been visiting her and her second husband in Montana and had not been ill, so his unexpected death was a terrible shock. She had found him in bed the morning after he had seemed well. The night before he had complained of being cold. I think Mildred was still in a state of disbelief. Her husband brought her to Fresno with furniture for her room in the condo.

Our new home was technically a planned unit development, but it was managed like a condo. We made only one change in the unit. The master bathroom door had to be widened. I could reach the light switches and move alone through the wide doors and halls. Semi-independence!

Mildred only stayed with us a short time. Mother encouraged her to attend the city college to study dental hygiene, a profession she was interested in. But she didn't want to go to school, didn't want to find a job, and most of all, she could not tolerate the Fresno heat. Her husband kept calling her and asking her to come home. Finally, she decided that she should return to Montana.

I was not sorry to see Mildred go. She seldom offered to help Mother and seemed to want Mother to wait on her. I felt that if I was supporting the three of us, the least she could do was to lighten Mother's load. We had little contact with her after she went back to Montana until another tragedy occurred that brought us together again. This time in Toledo.

In May of my third year at State we received bad news. Bob, now twenty-five-years-old, was awaiting surgery. His doctor in Toledo called Mother to explain the severity of his condition. He had broken his neck in a drug related diving accident. While intoxicated, he dove into the shallow end of a swimming pool. The doctor was not sure about the sequence of events between the accident and Bob's arrival at the hospital. She had scheduled surgery to relieve increasing pressure in Bob's brain.

Mother went to Toledo immediately to be with him. I was disgusted with Bob. He had never accepted responsibility for his actions. He had married too young and divorced his wife when their son, Charles, was an infant. Charles was four-years-old when this tragic incident occurred.

The doctor thought the outcome of the surgery would be positive. Mother stayed with friends until I came. My old boyfriend, Alan, a lawyer, thought she should have someone in the family with her. I called Mildred, explained the situation and asked if she could go. She agreed.

I stayed in Fresno to complete my end of the year duties. I felt I couldn't leave until I had prepared and administered the final exams in my three classes. As chair of the department and graduate student coordinator I took part in graduation. Then I flew into the Detroit airport and arrived in Toledo the next morning.

I was too late to say goodbye. Bob had died the evening before I arrived while they were changing his breathing tube. He had told the respiratory therapist that he didn't want to live his life as I had, in a wheelchair. His death, in my opinion, was a blessing. He knew he would not have been able to breathe without a ventilator. He was released from emotional and physical suffering and a life dependent upon drugs.

Mother was emotionally and physically spent. She was further devastated because when she and Mildred had been conversing the night before, Mildred suddenly exploded verbally. She told Mother that she was a horrible mother. I didn't probe into the details of their confrontation because it hurt Mother to discuss what happened. Mother didn't know what she had said to provoke Mildred's anger. It was now history, and we had much to do. We began to prepare for the funeral, notify the out-of-town family, etc. Our Pittsburgh and Chicago cousins came. I have not seen Mildred since that day.

A period of sadness engulfed us after Bob's death and our break with Mildred. We understood that in Bob's condition and emotional state he would not have adjusted easily to his cross. I prayed that he had asked for forgiveness of his sins before he died and that he was with His Heavenly Father who loves him as Mother did, unconditionally.

"…if you hold anything against anyone, forgive him, so that your Father in heaven may forgive you your sins."
MARK 11.25 (NIV)

With time Mother began talking about wanting to reconcile her differences with Mildred. Several years after Bob's death, I decided to write to her asking her to forgive us for whatever she thought we had done to harm her. Perhaps she resented the favoritism Dad and Mom exhibited toward me when we were young. She answered my letter by asking why we wanted to see her. Perhaps she thought I wanted her to care for Mother or me in the future. Nothing could have been further from my mind. We were planning for my retirement and our care. I replied that it would be nice to be able to gather as a family occasionally. We saw her daughter, Zo, once in a while and corresponded with her. Mildred did not answer this letter.

A Testing Period

Fresno was feeling more like home than any other place we had lived. Mother and I were building a family of friends we met at church and at the Newcomer's Club who were very caring. I was treated kindly by people I met on campus. The focus on antidiscrimination of women and the disabled, brought about by the Civil Rights Act of 1964, may have opened the hearts of folks I met at the University. The dean of my school was supportive of my efforts to gain tenure. My class schedule requests were granted, and I was able to teach earlier in the day to avoid the fatigue I experienced in late afternoon and evening seminars. Unfortunately, my energy level and the job expectations did not permit me to be active in the local Theta alum group.

With time, an administrator was assigned to coordinate services for disabled faculty on campus. My request through his office for a computer was supported strongly by our departmental secretary. She had been typing my course outlines, tests and correspondence. This auxiliary aid helped the whole department, because it increased secretarial time for the other faculty's work. I heard some people had complained that I was given "special" consideration. I became much more productive with this new tool, and that may have irritated some of the less energetic faculty on campus. But the work I was doing improved my teaching and that was my goal.

Sheryl, who had always seemed like a sister, wanted us to drive to San Francisco for all of the holidays. Like us, she and her husband had no other family in California. They thought their girls should be with family during the holidays, if possible. It was a long drive, and Mother I were both tired when we arrived. When the girls were little, beginning at ages five and six, they couldn't wait until I was in bed so that they could play in my chair. We watched them become cultured young ladies. We enjoyed our visits with Sheryl's family.

Often, conventions, special meetings and other professional activities took place in San Francisco. We stayed with Sheryl unless I was presenting or taking part in some way. Then we stayed in the main hotel where we could get around easily. Sometimes we took one or two other ladies along, and Sheryl entertained all of us in her home. Then Mother could go shopping or sightseeing while my colleagues took me to meetings. Two experiences introduced my friends to the type of barrier we had faced for twenty years.

In one luxurious hotel on Union Square my companion, Catherine, took me to five bathrooms before we finally found an employee's facility I could use. She couldn't believe that in such a place there would be so little thought given to the needs of disabled persons.

One convention held in an old hotel that was being renovated presented us with an amusing tale to relate. Judie, a friend who is not a speech-language pathologist and I checked in at the desk in the morning to ask if I could use a room at noon. According to the convention committee, the restrooms were not convenient for wheelchair users, but special arrangements would be made for convention participants. Their facilities were under construction to comply with the new governmental regulations. The desk clerk assured me that this would not be a problem and that we should come back before the lunch hour.

Judie went shopping and returned to help me at the agreed upon time. When we went to get the key for a room with an accessible bathroom, the desk clerk said they didn't have an empty room for me to use. I insisted that they accommodate me as promised. Finally, another man came to explain that he had arranged for me to use the men's bathroom in the bar. He would clear the space and stand outside the door to prevent anyone from entering. We followed him to the designated place. When we opened the door, we saw a marble wall between the toilets that blocked me from getting close enough to use either of them. We showed him the obstacle, and he said he had another idea to check out.

We waited while he collected several other people who led us single file through the main lobby. Now there were four of us following the leader. People watched us with interest. What was going on?

The group directed us to a restroom that had all but a few stalls removed. Women were inside combing their hair, etc.

The lady in the hotel group asked everyone to leave while I used the toilet farthest from the door. When we accomplished our goal, our "guards" went their separate ways. The next day we found this spot again without any fanfare. I have never gone back to this hotel, but I understand it is now fully accessible for wheelchair users.

During my tenure as chair of the department, the Education Department of the federal government invited me to review grant applications in Washington, D.C. Mother and I planned a lay-over in Pittsburgh where Bob's son, Charles, who lived in Toledo, often joined us to visit Mother's side of the family. We now had twenty years of experience dealing with steps at entrances in buildings, freight elevators, and airports. Other than scheduling flights in the winter foggy season, air travel had never been a problem. Even my flight alone into Detroit when Bob died went smoothly.

Airline personnel transferred me into an aisle chair in small planes. They lifted me into the nearest reserve aisle seat when my wheelchair could pass through the first class section. Sometimes we were given first class seats when they were available, and the plane was not sold out.

I have heard horror stories about the airline's handling of other disabled people, but I have none to relate. My weight, 100 to 110 pounds, made me an easy transfer for two people. The flight attendants or the airline staff who helped me always remarked about me being light as a feather or some similar comparison.

My five years as department chair seemed short because we were always traveling somewhere, in or out of state. The challenges I faced on campus were stimulating. Renovation of the old university training school cafeteria into a functional speech and hearing clinic was my biggest achievement. Although for five years I enjoyed being in charge, I knew the position did not bring out my best qualities. I was battling pride.

After disagreeing with the faculty on an important personnel decision affecting the future of our program, I faced a series of personal attacks. Marion, my closest friend and colleague, visited me at home and warned me that if I insisted on my stand, even though I was right, my position as chair would terminate. I could not relent nor compromise. I could not sacrifice my integrity, which meant more to me than any chairmanship. I couldn't let the students down by changing my position. The period of dissension proved to be most frustrating and stressful. I felt as though I were walking through fire. But God was actually carrying me through it.

"When you pass through the waters,
I will be with you;
and when you pass through the rivers,
they will not sweep over you.
When you walk through the fire,
you will not be burned;
the flames will not set you ablaze."
ISAIAH 43.2 (NIV)

That spring I was nominated to chair the University Academic Policy and Planning Committee. I had worked on this committee for two years and had the support of its members. A department chair could not also chair a university-wide committee so I took a leave from the department position. During my absence the faculty were responsible for the outcome of the personnel matter of the previous year. After struggling against them about this personnel issue, even though they agreed that I had made the right decision, I was no longer able to lead them. I returned to the classroom the next fall. I was not cut out to be a politician, a qualification for a position as an administrator at the college level. Nor was it possible for me to sacrifice quality programming if I could do something to strengthen the department. Teaching was my forte.

"So then, those who suffer according to God's will should commit themselves to their faithful Creator and continue to do good."
1 PETER 4.19 (NIV)

New Interests

Marion, my dear friend and colleague, anticipated changes in our professional role. She recognized the need for more cooperation between nurses and people in our field.

She and I prepared a convention program and taught several workshops on this topic. Soon two books that I edited evolved out of our new interest and need. They were titled *Nursing and the Management of Adult Communication Disorders* and *Nursing and the Management of Pediatric Communication Disorders* (1983, College-Hill Press).

Shortly afterwards, this excellent teacher left the department. We no longer had a person who was knowledgeable in the bilingual-biculturalism area.

Fresno had and still has a large Latino population and few Spanish-speaking speech-language pathologists (ASHA added *language* to the speech pathologist's professional title) and audiologists (specialists in hearing disorders) to serve these people. The American Speech-Language-Hearing Association was encouraging its members to learn another language and to prepare to diagnose and treat patients whose primary language is not English. If we wanted to support our profession in their goals, what was the best way to do it? Begin learning a second language, and encouraging our students to follow our example.

A New Challenge/Spanish

In 1979, I decided that I should learn to speak Spanish and prepare myself for communicating with the increasing population of Latinos in Fresno. Mother and I set off for Salinas, CA, that summer to attend a four week Adult School immersion class that Michelle, one of my former students recommended. We found a convenient reasonable motel near the school where we stayed during the week, and we drove back to Fresno for the weekend.

I knew two words of Spanish, "si" and "no." No English was spoken at the school, so from 8:30 in the morning until 3:30 in the afternoon we were in another country. My attempt to use my new language was a humbling experience. For the first time I used my wheelchair as an advantage. I didn't have to move when I didn't understand the directions that were given. Now I knew how my aphasic patients (post-stroke) felt when they couldn't comprehend what other people said and/or couldn't express their needs and desires.

In 1982, I asked for and was granted a leave-of-absence from the University. I had taken as many Spanish classes as I could during the school year and had attended two more summer sessions in Fresno of the same high quality instruction. After much study, I felt prepared to use my new skill as a professional tool. My goal was to study tests of speech and language available for hispanohablantes (Spanish-speakers).

By now I had enlarged my circle of Spanish speaking professional friends. We formed a study group that met weekly in my home. We were all fascinated by the language. I also felt led to initiate a weekly Spanish Bible Study for the university students under the guidance of a Spanish professor. Bill, a member of my study group played Spanish hymns on the piano, and some staff of InterVarsity Christian Fellowship joined us occasionally. We continued this activity for several years on campus and then in my home.

In 1984 my teaching efforts were rewarded. I was the recipient of the District V California Speech-Language-Hearing Association Outstanding Achievement Award in the Area of Academic Excellence at the University Level. My students, who were now working in the state, nominated me for this award.

"Lord, help me to always obey
when the lights of the world seem to blind me."
(<u>BE MY GUIDE</u>, SHANKS & UDE, 1982)

Another highlight of the early '80s was a period of writing religious lyrics to music Bill composed. We grew closer to the Lord through this experience. How rich my life had become!

Gatherings with Fresno disabled women also enriched my life during the eighties. Eight or ten of us met informally, usually in someone's home, to share solutions to problems we encountered.

Slowing My Walk

The Home Stretch

IN 1985 I WAS FACED with one of my biggest adjustments to my carefree life style. Mother fell and broke her hip and right shoulder. At the time I had a helper at school who knew my routine, but when I wasn't in school Mother not only cared for me but also managed our affairs and home. This all changed when she fell in our kitchen.

The accident happened when we returned home after an enjoyable evening with friends. Mother ran to answer the phone, and her heel caught on an exposed telephone cord. She couldn't free herself. When she hit the concrete floor, it sounded like a bomb was exploding. I called Virginia, a neighbor, and asked her to look for our house key that Mother had hidden in a bush in the front patio. Mother had locked the deadlock thinking we were in for the night, and I couldn't reach it. Virginia couldn't find the key. What was I to do? The horrible part was that she was groping through the bushes in a thunder storm.

I called Dr. Radding, our doctor, to explain the predicament I was in and ask his advice. If I called 911, they would break down the door, and I would be in an unlocked house all night. Dr. Radding was not available, it was Sunday, so I talked with the on-call physician. He didn't understand our situation and became angry because a half hour had passed since Mother fell. He said I either had to open the door in fifteen minutes or he would call the emergency number. Just then I heard, "I found it," Virginia had located the key! The doctor, finally realizing the problems I faced, called the paramedics for me and asked them to take Mother to the hospital. He would be there to take care of her.

Virginia, drenched from the storm, went with Mother to the hospital. Her husband, who was speechless from a stroke, stayed with me. I had to find someone who could help me immediately. I couldn't take care of my needs, and it was near my bedtime. I quickly called Melodie, my school helper, who offered to stay with me while Mother was in the hospital. What a relief! The Lord's peace was with me. He had provided everything I needed in this emergency. But who would be with us after that week?

"Do not be anxious about anything…
present your requests to God."
PHILIPPIANS 4.6 (NIV)

Mother was under the care of our wonderful doctor. I could not panic. Something would work out. I knew Sheryl couldn't help us. She had just opened a hat shop, Hats on Post, and had no one to relieve her. I called Pat, my Pennsylvania cousin, who had told Mother that she would come in a health crisis. She discussed the situation with her husband and decided she could not help us then.

Mother thought Pat would come. She told Dr. Radding we would have a family member with us when she went home. I knew he would not let Mother come home if I didn't have someone to help us. He would want her to go to a skilled nursing center where she could receive the special care she needed. But I knew that she would not get quality care in such an institution. I wanted her to be treated as she had treated me, like a queen.

Right then I resolved to solve this problem and keep my plan a secret. I would not tell the doctor nor Mother what I was going to do. We agreed that I should go to work every day instead of visiting the hospital. Mother had a phone in her room so that I could call her every few hours. She called me if there was something she wanted me to do. We talked at night and friends who visited her during the day kept me informed of her progress. The surgery on her hip was successful, and she healed quickly. Dr. Radding said that her shoulder would be functional in nine months' time.

I interviewed a recommended nursing service representative and scheduled around the clock help for us the following week when Mother was to be dismissed from the hospital. In the meantime, I told Pat not to call Mother until I was with her to tell her the arrangements I had made and to diminish her disappointment that we would be alone at home.

On Sunday, the day before her release, Bill picked me up to go to the hospital. Pat and my other cousins were going to call at 2:00. I couldn't believe my eyes, there sitting beside Mother was Sheryl! I began to cry. I now was relieved of the pent up sorrow I felt about Pat being unable to be with us. I had prayed for a way to tell Mother without making her feel slighted and unloved. Now the news poured out easily, and Mother accepted it in her usual gracious way. Sheryl had taken the train from San Francisco on her one free day and would return by train at five o'clock. All of the Pittsburgh cousins got together and called at two. They chatted with Mother who had accepted the arrangement for her homecoming. She agreed not to tell the doctor because she was eager to sleep in her own bed. No nursing homes for us! The day I had dreaded turned out to be joyous.

I was now in charge and had changed roles with Mother without too many problems. This temporary role change from care receiver to caregiver prepared me for my future responsibilities at home. We took each day one at a time, praying for the Holy Spirit's guidance. We were amazed at how the Lord sent just the right people to care for us and give us the support we needed.

During this time period I maintained my schedule at the University and Mother mended quickly. Our experience with professional caregivers was not satisfactory, and it was very expensive, so we began our adventure with helpers from the university student population. Our family was enlarged to include these angels God had sent to either grow with us or help us grow.

"For he will command his angels concerning you
to guard you in all your ways;"
PSALM 91.11(NIV)

Mother's recovery was remarkable. In nine months she was able to resume her duties except for transferring me into the car. But I knew our life needed to become more home-centered.

Susan, Mother fully recovered, and Margaret, who graduated from the Nursing Department at FSU. She spent a semester caring for us between classes.

I diminished my professional involvement and began to contribute meditations to *El Aposento Alto (The Upper Room),* a daily devotional in Spanish.[1]

Traveling became more difficult after 1985. Mother was less energetic. The fall had taken its toll. She decided to retire from being my traveling companion.

Now I had to cut down on my out-of-town professional obligations. No more grant reviews, no air flights to other states. Sheryl knew of my choice to attend a class in dialects being taught in San Francisco rather than going to my fortieth high school reunion in Ohio. She decided I must go to the reunion and told me to make arrangements for the weekend trip. She would be my companion and attendant. I was surprised that she could find someone to cover for her at the shop, but accepted her offer without hesitation.

We had a great time at all of the reunion activities, and we even went on the boat trip on the Maumee River to see the growth of the port. Our accommodations at Alan and Ellen's home were ideal, and Sheryl had time to visit with her friends while I was busy.

The convention hall where the class met for the main meeting was large with open branching rooms. We set up a table to chat with close friends in one of the branches. I don't like looking up at people all

---

1   See the list of meditations at the end of this book.

evening. This way people could sit and talk with me. No sore neck the next day!

At the end of the evening, Jim, the class president, announced that Sheryl and I won the prize for facing the most obstacles to come to the reunion. Evidently, many people didn't realize I was there because suddenly a long line of my classmates who wanted to see me began forming at the entrance to the room. I hadn't seen most of them since graduation forty years before. What a thrill to know how many people remembered me!

What were the obstacles we faced on this trip? The first problem arose when I went to the Fresno Airport boarding area to catch the plane for San Francisco where I was to meet Sheryl. The gate attendant told me I had to wait for the next flight because my scheduled plane was too small. The shuttle service used older planes. Sheryl planned to meet me at the airport in time to catch our plane to Detroit. Knowing her tendency to be late, I asked them to call her to explain the situation. She had an extra hour-and-a-half before I'd arrive in San Francisco. I was right, she was still at home and relieved to know we were running late.

My flight was announced a short time later. The plane looked like a kitty-car. How big had the other plane been that they scheduled me on? How did they plan to load me in this one?

I always asked that my chair be loaded in the luggage section on the plane so that I could be transferred into it immediately on arriving at my destination. Was there room for me and the chair? The opening to the plane was only large enough for one person. Two men carried me, fireman style. One supported me under my arms and the other my legs, and they lowered me into the seat closest to the door. They stored my chair behind the seat.

The shuttle landed in an open area because it was too small for the jet wings. The men there were ready for me and proceeded to unload me in the same fashion. I saw Sheryl watching from a window inside the second floor walkway. The flight attendant put me inside a ground floor door, where there were many steps, and left to find Sheryl. Finally, they arrived, just in time for me to go to the restroom and reach the area where they were loading our flight. Wow! It was a good thing we had those few extra minutes because this was early afternoon. Due to engine trouble we were delayed hours in San Francisco and didn't land in Detroit until midnight. Dana, my foster sister who picked us up, was patiently waiting for us.

The rest of our trip went smoothly, but I vowed never to fly out of Fresno again. I felt, and according to Sheryl, looked like a sack of potatoes being carried off the plane. If my helpers put one foot in the wrong place, my body would have been on the ground in pieces. 1988 was my final trip by plane.

But car travel was still on my agenda and I had places to go. Sheryl traveled with me in the state. She went with me to Los Angeles when the California Speech-Language-Hearing Association again recognized my professional contributions by naming me "Fellow" in 1989.

"Come before him with thankful hearts.
Let us sing him psalms of praise."
PSALM 95.2 (TLB)

In 1990 I studied our situation. Did I want to spend more time with Mother or continue carrying my heavy load at the University? I was eligible for retirement. Was it time to rest on my laurels?

I had become discouraged by the lack of departmental support for a new area of instruction in bilingualism. There were already too many required classes for our degree and low priority was given to my offering, "Testing in Spanish." As a result few students signed up for this class. In the future I would have to carry the class as an overload if the class were to be added to the already bulging curriculum.

Anyone who is familiar with the California State University system knows that a professor's load can be a killer. I decided to take early retirement in 1990 and requested two undergraduate classes each semester instead of the four classes I was teaching. The system allowed five years of teaching in this program. When I signed the new contract, I knew professors on early retirement would be the first to be laid off in a budget crunch.

The crunch came sooner than expected. In the fall of 1992 two temporary teachers in our department, sixteen professors in other departments, and I were laid off. What a blow!

"But O my soul, don't be discouraged.
Don't be upset. Expect God to act!"
PSALM 42.11 (TLB)

Mother had two bad falls in the next six months. The first time no bones were broken, but she fractured her other hip in the second fall.

*Jeanette, a FSU student at the time and now a
registered physical therapist, Mother and I returning
from an appointment with Mother's doctor.*

Again we had to have more help, but it was easier to
manage the recovery period. We were getting enough
practice to run our own caregivers' service. Now I,
who had always wanted children but had never borne
one, had from eleven to sixteen young people each
semester in my family of helpers. Each was special and
caring. How blessed we were!

"'Sing, O barren woman,…
because more are the children
of the desolate woman than of her
who has a husband,' says the Lord."
ISAIAH 54.1 (NIV)

I knew that the lay-off would have a message for me if I would just look for it. Was there another professional setting where God wanted to place me? I began to find out which community doors would be open and which ones would be closed.

A colleague suggested that I apply in the Department of Linguistics at Fresno City College, which I did. I called the supervisors in the local hospital clinics and schools. Because of my physical condition I was unable to work with patients with dysphagia (swallowing problems). These people needed to be fed and watched carefully for choking. I couldn't handle them. That closed the hospital doors.

The Dean of the Humanities Department at Fresno City offered me a Saturday class in Linguistics during the spring semester. Fresno Unified School District hired me as a speech-language pathologist. Carol, the supervisor, assigned me to a part-time position at the area school I requested. My life was evolving (or maybe revolving) into an exciting whirlwind of activity with people; adults beginning college and children with communicative disorders.

The faculty at the University had not forgotten me. They called me back to teach in the spring. But I made a big mistake. I did not pray before accepting the chance to return.

> *"We should make plans -*
> *counting on God to direct us."*
> **PROVERBS 16.9 (TLB)**

The atmosphere at the University was hostile. Students were unable to get into classes they needed and class size was unreasonably large. Professors were assigned classes that they either were unprepared to teach and/or didn't want to teach.

The last became my problem. I felt out of my realm in the graduate course I was assigned. And the undergraduate voice disorders seminar had forty-nine students. Previously, twenty-five had been the limit for this class.

Two weeks passed. I knew that I was unable to continue with my schedule. The students were suffering, and so was I. The already overloaded faculty wanted to help me, but I decided, after much prayer, that the best solution was to find a replacement who was acceptable for the graduate class. I continued teaching the voice disorders seminar.

Before Easter, 1993, Mother entered the hospital with congestive heart failure and a subsequent stroke. With the assistance of my already prepared family of helpers, I managed to continue teaching at the University and Fresno City. The Linguistics class was a delightful and positive experience. I survived at the University.

The End of an Era

I asked for a leave-of-absence from the University and notified the Dean at Fresno City that my one semester experience there would be my last. I was truly sorry because the students were challenging and the subject matter was stimulating to me.

In May I began a twenty-four hour job, I was the administrator of a skilled nursing service for one, Mother, in our home. We knew we were beginning the last period of our lives together.

Mother's only evident residual from the stroke was a loss of sight and minimal expressive aphasia (loss of recall of words). Each of several small strokes she suffered afterwards took a little more of her vision until she was almost blind. This affected our food preparation routine. I became the supervising cook. Surprisingly, many of our college-aged assistants had never prepared a whole meal in their lives, and I hadn't been in the kitchen in years. The doctor ordered a salt free diet that complicated matters. It was almost impossible to make unsalted food palatable to Mother. But we tried.

My most difficult task was teaching our caregivers how to handle Mother's catheter so that she would not have urinary tract infections. Her physical condition worsened as the months passed and problems arose that were difficult for us to cope with alone. We coped by adding extra hours to our caregivers' schedules as needed. We soon had twenty-four hour care.

At this time I sent in my formal resignation to the department. They were unable to hire my permanent replacement as long as I was considered part of the tenured faculty. No one pressured me to leave, but I knew the only fair thing to do was to close the door. I had a long productive career and was ready to retire.

Taking over the responsibilities of Mother's house was not easy. Every move I made to acquaint myself with the cupboards, closets, etc., was an intrusion into her territory. Anyone who has had to care for someone at this stage of life can sympathize with the pain involved in our almost complete role reversal.

Fortunately, we had the Talking Books for the Blind and Handicapped that filled our hours alone together with diversion. Our loyal friends visited us regularly, and there was always someone coming and going. The in-home nurses sent for follow-up were excellent and cheerful. Mother was alert and good company until the last minute of her life. As always she was keeping me in line, and she was playing her new role as counselor to our caring student helpers with enthusiasm. She helped me meet the challenges of each day. Her sense of humor showed through during the most trying times.

When Mother's physical condition began to deteriorate rapidly, I asked whether she wanted me to call Mildred and ask her to come to see her. She said that now it was too late to try to communicate with her. Too much time had passed for reconciliation. As always I respected Mother's wishes.

The last two months of Mother's two year illness seemed like a year. She could not sleep at night and always wanted to come into my room. I had to sleep sometime; twenty-four hour duty was too heavy for me. The last few nights she kept asking to talk with me. Her constant requests did not allow our student helpers, who slept in her room, to sleep. All were carrying heavy class loads. One helper had two jobs and another was completing her student teaching. When I offered to find substitutes so that they could stay home and sleep, each one said no thanks. They thought Mother would not be comfortable without them with her. That represented the attitude of all of our helpers. What a blessing they were!

The doctor ordered hospice services two weeks before Mother's death. Their staff complimented mine and made this nightmare period bearable.

About a week later I heard a knock on my bedroom door at midnight. Our helper had brought Mother in the room in her wheelchair. She wanted to talk. I was surprised at how alert she appeared for this time of night. This opened the scene for a "night to remember." The description of such a happening was included in the helpful booklet the hospice counselor had given us. Those approaching death often have a period of normalcy when their mental state is clear, and they can express themselves in understandable words when they previously were unable to communicate their thoughts.

For the next two hours I held Mother's hand, and we sang our repertoire of songs that included all of the music we had enjoyed in our home. We began to share memories of good times. At one point Mother, very seriously, said "You were a little devil, Susan."

The caregiver's eyes opened widely and she blurted out, "You were?" We had the best laugh we'd shared in many months.

I agreed that I was a handful, but surely I had mellowed through the years. "It took a while," she added, with the usual twinkle in her eyes.

Mother wound down as quickly as she had wound up and asked to return to her room. Her mission was completed. The memory of our time together was the taste of humor we needed to get through the difficult period ahead of us. Mother and I prayed that the Lord would take her out of her misery.

As I sat by Mother's bed the last day of her life, I thought of the morning's events. I wanted her struggle to end when she sat, or rather was held in a sitting position, on the side of the hospital bed after her bath.

The visiting nurse finished bathing Mother, braided her long tresses and dressed her in a dainty gown. Mother was smiling as usual, a twinkle in her eye.

The nurse said, "Martha, you look like a little girl." Mother seemed shocked by this comment. Unbelievingly, she said, "I DO?" That was the moment I wanted etched in my memory, the eternally "young" mother eager to greet each new day and its experiences.

But Mother was not young. At eighty-six, she was relatively unwrinkled, a superwoman who had cared for me forty-plus years. Given her druthers, Mother would have wanted to close the door of life at that moment.

That was not God's plan. The two hours after her bath were full of struggle for breath. We knew the end was near but didn't say goodbye. Our caregiver, Stacy, and I alternated reading the twenty-third Psalm, Mother's favorite, after the visiting nurse left. The Bible which Mother always read was lost until that morning. I found it among many objects put away to make room for hospital equipment, just in time to close the last page of Mother's life with her primary source of peace and rest.

"The Lord gave and the Lord has taken away;
may the name of the Lord be praised."
JOB 1.21 (NIV)

After her last breath, I left Mother's room feeling peaceful, too, but not rested. I had been sitting in my wheelchair for many stress-filled hours.

When the hospice nurse arrived, I was in bed. She went into Mother's room to prepare her for being moved and called the Neptune Society. Then she came into my room and asked if I wanted to see Mother before they picked her up. I said, "No," quickly.

Her face registered her surprise. Was I the first person who answered, "No," when invited to return to their loved one's room after death?

The negative reply was spontaneous. No need to think. I had accomplished my goal. For almost two years our home had been a skilled nursing facility staffed mainly by loving college students. They cared for Mother and me as if we were members of their families. For the first time in many months I was not needed to handle or supervise some task. The job was done. I had my memory of the wide-eyed woman in braids like a young girl waiting for the Lord to take her and leaving me in His care.

There was no need to say good-bye formally. The memory of our last moments together fills my heart until we meet again. What joy I feel knowing that I chose the appropriate time and manner to say good-bye to my loved one, when she was still alive.

Sheryl and her husband, Joe, came from San Francisco that night to be with me. Joe left the following morning, but Sheryl stayed and helped me talk through the plans we had made for this day. At Mother's request there was no funeral nor memorial service. She knew I was not up to the emotional strain of a gathering of mourners and neither of us was ever fond of ceremony or ritual. The Neptune Society disposed of her remains in the ocean near San Francisco.

Later I found Mother's favorite prayer book, *Prayers Ancient and Modern* (A.L. Grenfell, 1926), among her things. She had marked a prayer written by a ninety-year-old woman that seemed to be a favorite. Every line applied to her struggle with age and illness. The writer asked for "…courage and patience to bear the infirmities, privations, and loneliness of old age…," for help in fighting temptation to be "…exacting, selfish, unreasonable, irritable, and complaining…," for preservation of her "…mental faculties to the end…," for warmth in her heart and affections, for "…sympathy toward others in joy and sorrow…" and for "…gratitude for the love and forbearance of those around…" her. She asked to be prepared to face death fearlessly, trusting in God's promise to be with her as she passed through the dark valley, and to be received into His Kingdom.

These petitions have become part of my daily devotions. I observed through Mother's actions that her prayers were answered. She taught me that old age can be a joyful, satisfying, and fulfilling period of life if you walk with the Lord.

"...I will satisfy him with a full life and give him my salvation."
Psalm 91.16 (TLB)

As I read this story, I think that it really could be Mother's and not mine. Without her solid faith and prayers we never could have overcome the obstacles we faced during my educational strivings. I seldom did anything alone. Now my life would be very different.

No longer would I have an on-site sewing expert to assist me with difficult seams and with the design of new patterns for my suits and coats. No longer would I have a knitting partner to finish new lap robes for the Gap Ministries (Nursing Homes). No longer would Bill, my piano-playing friend, and I have a humorous critic of our duets. No longer would I have an editor for my writing attempts. No longer would I have an objective listener to evaluate troubling situations. No longer could I receive instant encouragement when experiencing success and support when facing failure. No longer could I rely on the wisdom of someone who recognized my strengths and weaknesses when weighing the pros and cons of a decision. Mother wore so many *hats* in my life that it would take many people to take over the tasks she performed so well.

But Mother had taught me to live independently, and now I had to begin to put what I had learned to practice. How would I structure my life? I knew I would be very lonely without Mother.

*"Turn to me and be gracious to me,
for I am lonely and afflicted."*
PSALM 25.16 (NIV)

Was I equipped to handle my aloneness? If I called out, Mother would never answer me again. I was alone! I needed a plan to keep from slipping into a state of debilitating grief.

One of my first solutions to loneliness came from my experience in the field of education. Many classrooms have stations where the children work at a variety of topics. At times the teacher schedules children to work at stations of need, such as an additional reading lesson. Sometimes the children select a station of interest; they listen to music or to a recording of a humorous story.

I began to evaluate my interests and hobbies. What type of work areas or stations could I set up?

Because of my wheelchair, the stations had to be convenient and accessible. My design had to allow me to move from one station to another with ease. Fortunately, the condo could accommodate several stations. I faced the challenge with eagerness and soon was ready to battle my aloneness.

I began my war to combat loneliness and live as Mother wanted me to, happy and productive.

Whenever I became lonely I decided which of my activities would be fun and went to that station. I moved my piano, "my music station," to the kitchen near the window where the garden is in full view. My TV, knitting and sewing stations are nearby. The computer station where I write is now in the guest room. My "flower" station where I keep boxes of dried flowers to use in making greeting cards is set up there.

I don't put anything away at a station until I finish a project. Then I replace my materials with what I need for another. I just finished decorating a doll house for visiting children to play with. I used wall paper sample books and pictures from a Penney's catalog plus a set of furniture from a local thrift shop for my interior design.

My letter writing station is in the hall where I wait for my caregivers. A chest in the entrance way is the hiding place for my stationary and stamps.

I haven't set up a particular spot for devotions. My prayer station is wherever I am seated at the moment. As I move around the house I am aware that the Holy Spirit is always with me. When I think of this great gift I cannot feel lonely.

Friends and my family of helpers began to assume some of Mother's roles. With them and the projects I started, my life began to be stimulating and full again. I held on to the Lord's Promise that He would never leave me nor forsake me (Hebrews 13.5) and stepped forward into my new life.

I also felt Mother's presence in the house. After six years I still received her direction when I made decisions. I call this the *"nudge."* Do you ever feel as if someone is giving you a gentle push or trying to get your attention? That may be the nudge of your loved one.

Recognizing *"the nudge"* has been important to me in adjusting to my life without Mother – my best friend and counselor. Sometimes in quiet moments while reading the Bible or waiting for my caregiver, I suddenly get the feeling that I should call Mother's old friend. I don't want to call her because of the way she neglected Mother during her last days, but I feel a nudge from Mother. A nudge means do it!

I have had many of these feelings since Mother died. As many people who have lived together for a long time, I read Mother's mind. I knew how generous, kind, and forgiving she was. That was the way she acted, and that was how she wanted me to be. She always considered the feelings and shortcomings of other people. I am less like her than I would like to be. So when I feel the urge to do something good, *the nudge,* I think Mother is directing me from afar. Her nudges are very important to me and I act on them.

The power of the nudge is truly amazing and awesome. When I respond to the nudge, my life is enriched by memories of the old relationship I shared with my loved one.

Walking as God's Servant

My Ministry

"Set your minds on things above,
not on earthly things."
COLOSSIANS 3.2 (NIV)

As I SAT WITH MOTHER during her last days, I felt helpless. Not because I was in a wheelchair, but because I wanted to help her endure the long, painful days and especially the evenings, when we were alone. Friends and pastors who visited us and prayed for our well-being were a special blessing. But it was difficult for me to pray. I lacked an adequate resource to provide us with comfort and hope.

This experience led me to assemble Bible verses for other patients and their families to share during their last precious moments together. I had found God's work for me!

I typed a rough draft of my booklet of hope and prayed about how to copy it in a readable format. God provided the materials to produce my work. Cathy, one of my helpers, offered to lend me her Macintosh (Mac) computer with different fonts during the Christmas break. It had a friendly program that I learned quickly. I re-typed the booklet in English and Spanish in four weeks and had a thousand copies printed.

> "Sing out his praises! Bless his name.
> Each day tell someone that he saves."
> **PSALM 96.2 (TLB)**

Facing Death with HOPE, the title of my collection, and a Spanish version of the booklet became the focus of my service. My wish was to share God's promises with the dying and their families. Scriptures included were about relief from suffering, about God's forgiveness, about His compassion and about eternal life. Because I had terminated my teaching job at the University during Mother's illness, I had time to spread His Word through the booklets.

How was I to reach families struggling with a terminal illness? God showed me the way. Vickie, a librarian at a local medical library found a list of free-standing hospices in the United States. I began to mail out copies of the English booklet to chaplains and social workers associated with these agencies.

Distribution of the booklets to as many hospices as possible became my goal. Five years later I had sold or given away over six thousand of the English copies and two hundred and fifty of the Spanish. Hospices in twenty-one states have bought these booklets.

> *"Publish his glorious acts throughout the earth.*
> *Tell everyone about the amazing things he does."*
> **Psalm 96.3 (TLB)**

My next publication was inspired by Peggy Brandon, coordinator of the Fresno Gap Ministries. Peggy took a copy of *Facing Death* to one of the nursing home residents she visited. This woman had lost her favorite prayer book, which she treasured. She wanted something to replace it. Peggy began looking and was unable to find a small prayer book with large print at our local religious bookstore. *Facing Death* wasn't exactly what she was looking for, but it was something to give peace to this woman and other seniors.

This experience led me to begin writing *Prayers for Seniors*, a collection of sixteen short prayers. I printed them on my twenty-year-old computer and gave the rough copy to Peggy for her friend.

Several months later I gave a copy of *Prayers for Seniors* to another friend, Judie, whose mother-in-law,

Helen, was not well. I thought she might find the prayers comforting. She encouraged me to have them published in the same format as the first booklets on HOPE. Now I would have to rent a Mac computer because Cathy, who had loaned me hers before, had moved out of town.

A young couple, Moira and Javier, stopped in to ask how things were going. I related how I was calling around to compare prices for renting a Mac to prepare the new booklet. God sent a message to them on the spot! They offered to loan me their computer that was boxed up in preparation for their move to another apartment. I began typing the booklet and completed the task in the two weeks they were settling in.

"Great is Thy faithfulness!
...All I have needed Thy hand hath provided."
(GREAT IS THY FAITHFULNESS.
CHISHOLM & RUNYAN, 1972)

I used large print, font 18, which was easily read without my glasses. Again I had one thousand of the booklets printed and began my marketing task. Word of mouth and including them in my hospice mail-outs were my main methods of distribution. I had sold over a thousand by the year 2000 and was on the second printing of the booklet. God, who provides the resources for my work, also puts them in the hands of those seniors who need them.

> *"Even in old age they will still produce fruit and be vital and green."*
> **PSALM 92.14 (TLB)**

As I worked on these projects I felt Mother's presence in the house. Her nudge encouraged me to search the Bible for verses to punctuate my thoughts and to grow in my faith. God, as usual, had a special surprise for me when I finished the Seniors booklet.

Gene, a recently retired Christian colleague and his wife, Nancy, visited me with a prayer request. I gave them a copy of each of my booklets and explained how God had provided the resources for the projects. The next day Gene called and offered to give me his old Mac. They were going to buy a new one and thought God had spoken to them about my need through their visit. Praise Him!

> *"Praise God from whom all blessings flow;..."*
> **(PRAISE GOD, FROM WHOM ALL BLESSINGS FLOW,**
> **KEN & BOURGEOIS, 1972)**

Flower Inspirational Cards

The Mac opened up another ministry for me. I had been making greeting cards with dried flowers for several years. Now I began decorating them with flowers and Bible verses using different fonts. Everyone thought they were beautiful.

Because I was having trouble with my back I couldn't continue to knit lap robes for the Gap Ministries. What else could I do for those seniors who were not able to stay at home like I was?

I called Peggy at Gap and invited her to come and see the flower cards. I knew that the Gap budget was small. Could they use my cards? I offered to make as many cards as I could each month for them to send as birthday cards to the elderly they visit in nursing homes. Peggy also wanted to give them as thank you cards for their volunteers. In 2000 I also began making cards for the chaplain at a local hospice. God blesses me when I make these cards. I give thanks that I am in my home and enjoying life with loving caregivers and friends around me.

Blessings to Share

Writing became much more exciting now that I had my own Mac. Through prayer God directed me into another project to express His love.

Kathy Kramer-Howe, a bereavement counselor at a hospice in Phoenix, Arizona, wrote to ask that I "nurture" the idea of compiling a little book of blessings. She was using *Facing Death* with her patients. I began collecting Bible verses and writing blessings to accompany them in 1997. *Blessings for Sunrise to Sunset,* the working title of this new work, was changed to *Blessings for Sunrise to Sunrise* to reflect the twenty-four hour a day need for blessings. All who care for a growing family or for people who are ill know days don't end at sunset. In the '90s we live and work around the clock.

I realized that asking for God's blessing is a part of many people's prayer pattern. In many cultures the daily blessing of family members when they go to bed or leave home is a custom. Another custom is to ask God to bless our food to strengthen our bodies. Families give their blessing to their children when they decide to marry and as part of the celebration of the marriage. The clergy bless crops, animals, babies at baptism, couples being joined in matrimony, and the dying.

I also knew that while verbally gifted folks find it easy to bless others in public, some people have little practice in praying aloud. They are shy about sharing their love for others by blessing them. My collection of blessings is for people who want to begin to incorporate blessings into their prayer life. They may also be appropriate for the experienced counselor or chaplain who blesses people every day but wants a blessing for a special occasion.

Blessings for Sunrise to Sunrise contains situational blessings appropriate for all who are walking through the various stages in the life cycle. I also included blessings for helping people lean on or find God as they pass through both turmoil and illness. A few are for festive occasions.

In January 1999, after sending the Blessings booklet to friends as my Christmas card, I began praying for guidance. How was I to continue to spread God's message of love and hope? A bereavement counselor in Texas, who gives my *Facing Death with HOPE* to families of patients entering her hospice program, called me. She asked if I had something similar for families grieving the death of their loved one. Her call was an answer to my prayer for my next project for the Lord.

I immediately began reading Christian literature on grief and found that no inspirational guide had been published in my style, short and simple. The format evolved into *Facing Grief with HOPE*. This booklet has sold much faster than the others. It was needed! A friend encouraged me to translate this work into Spanish. In 2001 I finished this project and began to market it. What I write next is presently in God's plan, not mine.

A Reassuring Message

In 1985 when Mother broke her hip and shoulder in a fall involving a wicked telephone cord, she and I began to talk about our future. We knew it was a question of time until Mother could no longer be my main caregiver.

> *"A prudent man foresees the difficulties ahead and prepares for them;..."*
> **PROVERBS 22.3 (TLB)**

We visited a local home for the aged managed by a Catholic order of nuns. Impressed by the pleasant surroundings and caring atmosphere, we requested future admittance to this lovely refuge. Our names were put on their very long waiting list. The Mother Superior told us to contact her when, and if, we wanted to move to their home.

After Mother died in 1995, I visited the Catholic home again. The bereavement counselor associated with the hospice team that served us during Mother's last days advised me not to make any lasting decisions until a year had passed. I was encouraged to remain in my home.

My student caregiver and I toured the residence again while waiting for the Mother Superior. I could see that all the people living there looked as though they were in their eighties, at least. Most had lived twenty or more years longer than I had. I returned home determined to work out an independent living plan.

Actually, I had been managing everything at home for two years. But I had not had time to become aware of my skills in this area. Now was the time to discontinue my reactive life style and change my pace to a slower beat of my drum.

As head of household I now became concerned about the condition of my house. The hall walls looked like a truck had passed through them every day. During her illness Mother was determined to move her own wheelchair as long as she could. She was nearly blind from her recurring strokes and was running into everything. She told me to paint after she died and not to worry about how the house looked in the meantime. As always, she was right. She needed to maintain her independence as long as possible.

Now it was time to erase the memories of her struggle. Painting over the walls of pain became priority number one.

Each household task that had been put on hold for several years was added to my list of work to do. Soon a new roof on the house was in place. I had a new hot water heater installed before the original one gave out. Mother's room was converted to an office.

In 1997 I couldn't believe two years had passed since I made my decision to stay in place for a while. I was managing well living independently and my general health was excellent. But my peers were facing surgeries and hospitalizations for major and minor problems, and I lacked a plan for such an emergency. I didn't have family in Fresno, and none of my friends could put their lives on hold while they cared for me. Only a few of my helpers were nursing majors. What would happen if I were taken to the hospital and dismissed while still requiring nursing care? Shuffling the schedules of my flexible college aged caregivers had become routine for me. I had forgotten that someone would have to take over this chore if, or when, I could no longer do it. I had to face reality. A plan had to be put together quickly. I began to pray for guidance in my planning.

Could I be admitted to the Catholic home on a temporary basis when ill or after a hospitalization? I called to schedule another conference with their new Mother Superior. She began by asking me who had cared for me in the past. How had I kept my mother at home through her long illness until the moment of her death?

The Mother Superior listened intently to my explanations. After I had finished she looked at me wonderingly. She asked why, if God had cared for me for so many years, would I expect Him to abandon me now? The truth behind her question stunned me.

"Reassure me that your promises are for me,
for I trust and revere you."
PSALM 119.38 (TLB)

What a timely reassuring message God had sent me through this servant! He had led me to this refuge at precisely this moment so that I would hear these words of wisdom.

Of course, He would not leave my side in an emergency. If I needed a temporary home, He would provide that too.

Almost a year passed and another local Christian home opened its infirmary to outpatients. At my request their nurse coordinator visited me to discuss the services they offered. After much prayer, I contacted David, a young, trustworthy Certified Public Accountant I had known for years. Would he manage my business in case of a sudden illness? After I explained my needs, he agreed to help me. God's plan evolved. I felt His continued protection as I faced the unknown future.

> *"Listen to this wise advice; follow it closely,...*
> *pass it on to others: Trust in the Lord."*
> **PROVERBS 22.17-19** (TLB)

The Greatest Challenge:
Living God's Word

The potential of serving in another ministry at home became evident when Mother no longer could care for me. The Lord began sending us people to fill our needs. Marvell, the secretary of our church, came to the house to cut our hair. Gary, a university student from InterVarsity Christian Fellowship drove me to and from work. But our helpers were not all Christians. Often they did not go to church or have knowledge of Christianity.

Our main source of help continued to be the University where I could hire students from a variety of majors. Many of our workers were in physical therapy, and some were specializing in education and in business. But they all had a heart for helping others, especially seniors, and they all ministered to us by teaching us patience. We shared their problems and triumphs. How they blessed us!

> *"...I urge you to live a life worthy
> of the calling you have received."*
> **EPHESIANS 4.1** (NIV)

I asked myself, "How can I be a blessing to all who come to my home?" Being a blessing became my new and most difficult ministry. Every day I try to be an example of Christian love. I'm challenged to project the fruits of the spirit through my words and actions ("kindness, patience, gentleness, peace, goodness, joy, faithfulness, self-control" Galatians 5.22-23). Regardless of the circumstances, I want to witness my faith. My daily prayer time is focused on asking for guidance. How can I achieve God's goals?

I feel God will base my final accounting on the positive rather than the negative aspects of my example. I pray for strength to be what He wants me to be and to grow and harvest in love and faith.

"I will try to walk a blameless path,
but how I need your help,
especially in my own home,
where I long to act as I should."
PSALM 101.2 (TLB)

Witnessing in Trouble

An opportunity to witness my trust in the Lord to my caregivers came early in the year 2000. February 9th, two weeks after I had gum surgery, I awakened with severe vertigo, which I called "The Washing Machine Syndrome." I felt as if I were the clothes. This was my first major health crisis since polio, and I was alone. But of course I wasn't, God was with me.

My situation was complicated by the fact that my doctor and her associates had just notified everyone under their care that they would not treat patients who were covered by a specific HMO insurance company, mine, after May 1st. Other insurance companies they *would* accept were listed in the letter.

When I received this news I began searching for a new physician who would treat me with my present insurance. The open enrollment period for retirees to make insurance changes had just passed. I would have to wait from May to January without insurance if I stayed with my present doctor. No way could I do this. Also, if other doctors in town were canceling patients with my insurance, I might not be able to find one who would take me if I waited until May. I called the insurance company and asked how to make an immediate change.

Through friends I heard about a Christian physician who, when I inquired, accepted me with my HMO coverage. The receptionist told me he wanted to see new patients before he treated them. That was not a problem, I thought, so I decided to wait for the Easter vacation when one of my helpers could take me for a physical. I was healthy, hadn't been sick in years. What a mistake!

Although I was relieved to know I had a new doctor, two weeks later I faced the health crisis, the *vertigo*. My attack occurred when I was still under the care of doctor number one. When I called to ask what to do, the nurse relayed the doctor's message to report back the next day if the symptoms had not subsided. I began having other symptoms which suggested a stroke and heart attack, so I called again. This time I was sent to the Emergency Room of the hospital. It was difficult to examine me in her office, she said, because of their high tables and lack of people to lift me.

My experienced caregiver managed to transfer me into the car and off we went to the hospital. The ER physician said I had benign positional vertigo or labrynthitis, or both. My heart and all vital signs were normal. A Dramamine infusion relieved my nausea condition somewhat. I was sent home with anti-vert medicine, which would diminish my nausea, and was told to rest. As soon as possible I should make an appointment with my primary care doctor and/or an otolaryngologist (specialist in ear, nose, and throat). We were home by midnight, and I slept well in my own bed.

I felt better for several days and then had another attack, worse than the first. Now I needed help all of the time and my caregivers only worked certain hours a day. It was time to get into gear and think and pray. I knew what I had to do, follow the emergency plan I had outlined previously. The next evening I decided this was not a two or three day illness, something had to be done quickly while I could still do it.

> *"Lord, when doubts fill my mind,*
> *when my heart is in turmoil,*
> *quiet me and give me*
> *renewed hope and cheer."*
> **PSALM 94.19** (TLB)

My first step was to call the home health care agency I had contacted before. They had a four hour waiting time to begin service. The person who answered the phone said, "Home Health," and hung up. After this happened three times, I used my disabled phone line and asked the operator to try the call. They hung up on her too. Then she asked me to stay on the line while she called again. Somehow she got through for me. The receptionist told me it would take a week to find people to care for me and recommended that I call back the next day. I knew this was a dead end. I had to have help immediately. What was I to do?

Next I called to explain the situation to each of my helpers. They agreed to expand their hours to equal twenty-four! Thank God I could stay at home.

Had I witnessed during the first step of my crisis? I think so because my day helper told me she couldn't believe how calm I was while preparing for my trip to the ER. This was my second trip, the first was in 1949 when I had polio. Was God preparing me for the end of my life or another beginning? Time would tell.

I was to make a third trip to the ER in a week. The tide turned again, for the worse. I called the new doctor for an appointment because I now had a fever. The nurse reminded me that the physician wouldn't treat me until I had my physical. She directed me to his group's urgent care center. So far my caregiver was still able to load me in the car with the help of a friend who went with us.

The physician in charge prescribed antibiotics and a decongestant, now I had ear and sinus infections. No more anti-vert, he said. We stopped at the pharmacy for the medication and I was in such a hurry to get into bed that I took the pills without reading about the side effects. Guess what they were? Dizziness and nausea!

The next day when I could not move my eyes or head without being very ill, I read the directions. I didn't take another pill, you can be sure of that! But I did call the doctor's office and they referred me to the ER again. This time I had to be transported by ambulance. The ER physician put me on anti-vert again. No decongestant this time.

I was sent home but was completely bed bound. None of my caregivers was in nurses' training; they would have to be taught how to care for me in bed. I had not used a bed pan for fifty years and spent as little time in bed as possible.

At this point my teaching skills came in handy. As each helper arrived I initiated a speedy nurses' aid seminar starting with vocabulary such as (1) fracture pan (a small bed pan used by people who have broken a leg or hip), (2) chuck (a disposable pad to protect the bed), (3) a draw sheet (a piece of sheet put under me where I am heavy to move me on the bed), etc.

I scheduled the caregivers so that one person stayed a few minutes after her shift and the next person arrived a few minutes early. That way two people were on hand to help me out of bed and in the restroom. One held me up in the chair to prevent me from falling, and the other transferred me from the wheelchair to the toilet. We got into some funny positions, which brought on laughter, but my method worked. I canceled one girl because she didn't clean bathrooms and would have been hesitant to help with the fracture pan. She didn't complain!

In the next three days I had a trained family of caregivers who were performing their tasks like veterans. No helper was absent or late during this crucial time of my illness.

I began to heal slowly, but spent most of the time in bed for ten days. Finally, I could sit up for more than five minutes at a time and eat a regular diet.

When I was up and about, I scheduled a physical with my new doctor. He was warm and competent. He put me on more medication because the sinus infection was still not cleared up and referred me to an ear specialist, who also turned out to be another caring person.

The diagnosis of positional vertigo in my right ear was confirmed by testing, and the Epley maneuver, a method to treat my condition, was carried out two times, ten days apart. I was relieved somewhat, but after six months I still had vertigo occasionally. A hearing loss in my left ear was also detected. Did this mean that I had two problems? The doctor said the results of future hearing testing may answer this question. He recommended that I eliminate salt, chocolate, and other sources of caffeine from my diet. I was also told to avoid alcohol, no problem for me.

I followed these instructions and the fullness I felt in my ears slowly disappeared. At the time of this writing I have not experienced any severe vertigo for eight months. Praise God!

As I regained my strength during the next few weeks I would have many more opportunities to demonstrate my faith. I asked myself, "How would Jesus react in my circumstances?" and tried to witness His Way. Was I successful? I hope so.

I had learned that I could experience a serious health crisis and still remain in my home. I felt sure the new doctors would follow my progress with interest. During my last visit my new primary physician told me that he and his staff would take good care of me; no other doctor had ever given me that assurance. I was grateful for healing under his and the Lord's care. God had continued to provide for me abundantly.

> *"Though I am surrounded by troubles,*
> *you will bring me safely through them."*
> **PSALM 138.7** (TLB)

Evaluating the Past

In contemplating how Mother and I managed to do what we did, I'd say the keys were prayer and work.

We were a team – Jesus, Mother and I. Throughout my adult life God gave me the gift of *hope* which always had His promises as the base. And of course, the encouragement of many people sparked the spirit of risk-taking required to make changes. Often a positive listener prompted a decision at a turning point that led me into the next exciting stage of my journey.

Space does not permit me to tell about many friends' and our family of caregivers' contributions during difficult periods. But those people not mentioned here have their names written in *The Book* which is more important than being named in mine.

> *"I will sing to the Lord*
> *because He has blessed me so richly…"*
> **Psalm 13.6** (TLB)

As the first part of *Chosen…* ends, I think that my life will continue according to God's map for my walk. Did God want me to write about my experiences as I walk in faith? He probably would expect me to step forward and relate other ways He would bless me in the future and lead me to continue to serve others. Where He leads I will follow.

2001–2012

Continuing to Serve

AT THE END OF 2001, the songs of praise I was singing reflected my attitude as I faced my future course with hope. A flower card I made with the reminder "God who has provided in the past will continue to provide in the future" was placed in a prominent spot on my dressing table. My *Friend* is always with me.

> *"Why should I feel discouraged?*
> *Why should the shadows come?*
> *Why should my heart be lonely,*
> *and long for heav'n and home,*
>   *when Jesus is my portion?*
>   *My constant friend is He,*
>   *His eye is on the sparrow,*
>   *and I know He watches me."*
> **(HIS EYE IS ON THE SPARROW,**
> **MARTIN & GABRIEL, 1905)**

I was certain that when God chose me, He not only prepared me for His work, but He also charted when and how I would accomplish it. I knew He would comfort me at stressful times. My heart is at peace because I know that He is in charge of my life and His timing is perfect.

My immediate plan was to focus on the promises in the Psalms and the Scriptures in the New Testament. I knew my ministries would evolve because nothing is carved in stone. The future chapters in my life may not seem to be as exciting or productive as those that I have lived through, but I know that I will be doing what God has prepared me to do. I will grasp every opportunity to use my talents to encourage others.

God, the Potter, will mold me each day. One step forward, sometimes two backward, but with the goal to give honor and glory to His name. I will try to...

"Be joyful always;
pray continually; give thanks
in all circumstances,..."
1 THESSALONIANS 5.6-18 (NIV)

As I began to look back, I counted six years of my successful trial period to live independently after Mother's death. We still had the weekly sessions of my Spanish conversation group. We had become a "family."

The Village Readers continued to meet in my home monthly. The books we read provoked much discussion.

Friends still called and visited me to enrich my life. My caregivers were loyal and stimulating. I was able to keep the household running smoothly and was enjoying life to the fullest. I'm sure Mother was nudging me from Heaven when I needed her advice.

I was entering a different period in my life, full of many challenges and blessings.

Problems with vertigo led to a discovery of a need for a radical change in my diet. Adjusting to a "new me" due to aging and the post-polio syndrome was sometimes difficult. I had to leave my home temporarily because of a fire, but the outcome was positive. I will explain what happened during this period of my life in a separate section of this book.

> *"Always give yourselves fully*
> *to the work of the Lord,*
> *because you know that your labor*
> *in the Lord is not in vain."*
> **1 Corinthians 15.58 (NIV)**

In 2002 my Christian ministry expanded. The completion of another HOPE booklet kept me productive. I accepted a bigger challenge, to write a book describing my years of success hiring caregivers. If using your brain keeps seniors from having Alzheimer's, I was sweeping out the cobwebs associated with the disease daily.

The following sections of *Chosen* will present more details about my life. Read on and you will see that it has never been dull.

Rejoicing with my "Spanish Family"

SINCE I BEGAN TO STUDY Spanish in 1979, my life has been enriched beyond the classroom. I had no idea of the adventures it would lead me into – traveling to Mexico to study while living with a family and thirty years watching families solve problems during the weeknight telenovelas (soap operas).

I am still working on my comprehension of Spanish through watching the nightly news in Spanish and the telenovelas. This skill has enabled me to converse with the many wonderful, caring Spanish speaking caregivers I have been able to employ.

At the end of the fourth University Spanish intensity class I was enrolled in, I wanted to practice speaking the language and learn more vocabulary. I had made many friends in the classes who felt the same way. I invited them to come to my home once a week for an hour or two of conversation. Most of the people in the group were teachers of Bilingual classes or English as a Second Language (ESL). In the fall our group became smaller when they went back to work. Marilyn, an

ESL teacher who has become like a sister to me, and Imogene, another loving friend, continued to attend the weekly get-togethers. When Imogene's husband retired, she moved south and we only communicated by mail.

Marilyn and I continued to meet for years. Then Jeannette, my former caregiver and Spanish classmate, joined us when she moved back to Fresno after being married. Bill, Linda and Ann, three people who were enrolled in the University intensive program, retired and became part of our group again. I found Ron, an insurance claims agent, through an article in the San Diego newspaper about the Spanish class we attended in Ensenada. Imogene sent me the article knowing we wanted more enthusiastic people in our group. Ron fit into our group quickly. Ransom, the retired University Spanish teacher who led the Spanish Bible study I organized on campus in the late '80s, began coming after his wife's death. He was then ninety-four and soon celebrated his ninety-fifth birthday with us. All but two are retired teachers who want to practice their Spanish and learn more vocabulary.

The group had grown from two to nine persons by 2012. We are like a family. Each person is supportive of the others. In fact, I consider them my Fresno "family." I was comforted by them during the years when Mother was so ill.

Our meetings don't follow any strict format. At 7:30 p.m. we begin talking about the events of the week, the health of family members who are not well and trips taken by someone in the group. If the travelers have pictures taken on their trips, they bring them and we pass them around and ask questions about them. That night is a regular travelogue. We share like a real "family."

At around 8:20 we read aloud several pages or a chapter from a children's book in Spanish. Edy, a librarian who comes to practice with us when she can, checks out nine copies of the book so that we each have a copy. We can keep them as long as it takes us to read them. Sometimes it's months before we finish one book because we look up words we don't know. There are often many new words depending on the subject.

We discuss the differences between the book and the same book in English or the movie of the story. For example, many Spanish chapters of the *Wizard of Oz* were not included in the English movie.

We laugh a lot during this "reading practice." We stop at 8:45 except when we have birthday parties.

We schedule three or four birthday parties each year, usually for several people whose birthdays are close together. Everyone brings the funniest cards they can find for the celebrants.

My eightieth birthday party was the most spectacular event of my life. Jane, a Villager friend, hired a local folk singer to entertain us. Paul and Karen, colleagues from Fresno State, sent me eighty roses. That was awesome! The picture below shows me ready to blow out the candles before cutting my cake.

Marilyn and I celebrating my 80th birthday with our Spanish "family."

For birthday number eighty-one, Jane surprised me again by bringing three retired Afro-American sisters who sang the songs of the forties and fifties to entertain us. They were terrific!

I didn't want to celebrate my eighty-second, but again Jane said she had a surprise for me. She brought a high school Spanish teacher who sang many Spanish songs accompanying herself with her guitar. We joined her when we knew the song. The neighbors probably wondered what was going on when they heard our *Ai Ai Ai Ai celito lindo…*

I look forward to this "family" continuing to join me as long as they can and feel blessed as they demonstrate their love for me.

One evening while talking with my cousin, Pat, who lives in Pennsylvania, I explained how my Spanish speaking friends help with the monthly raffles of the clearing house items. She had never heard about this before and asked, "What is the clearing house? What do you raffle?" My explanation to her will be told in the next section of the book.

Establishing a "Clearing House"

"I needed clothes and you clothed me…"
MATTHEW 25.36 (NIV)

BEFORE MOTHER'S DEATH SHE AND I talked about what she wanted me to do with her belongings. I was to pick out what I wanted and give the rest to family and our "caregiver family" who wanted something to remember her. I was not to donate her things to an agency where they would sell them.

At that time we had twenty-four caregivers. Many were students at Fresno State and most were from large, struggling families.

With this thought in mind, I displayed everything in Mother's room like a clothing store and invited the helpers and some close friends to a "Clearing House" opening. It was a successful and joyful event. Mother would have been pleased with the outcome – an empty room and smiling faces.

When my cousin Sheryl's Aunt Kay (who lived in Fresno) died, I opened the clearing house again. Sheryl and Anne, her daughter, came to Fresno from San Francisco to empty Kay's apartment.

Sheryl posted some FOR SALE signs in the apartment building's elevators and people came to buy some of the heavy furniture. She gave many items she didn't want or couldn't sell to my caregiver, Magdalena, who had a large family.

Kay was a compulsive shopper/buyer. Some of her clothing still had price tags. Sheryl asked if I would call an agency to take away what was left in the apartment.

As you might imagine, I didn't do this. Jerry, my Saturday caregiver, and my friend, Diana, loaded their cars four times to take everything that was left in Kay's closets, kitchen and bathroom to my condo.

We stored the large pieces like the ironing board, lamps, etc., whatever didn't fit in a car, in the garage of Diana's daughter, Peggy, who lived across the street from the apartments.

The next day Jerry borrowed his brother's truck and took everything from Peggy's garage and put it in the garage at my condo.

"You have been a refuge for the needy…"
ISAIAH 25.4 (NIV)

After my garage was organized, the knickknacks were placed on tables in my house and the clothing was displayed in my extra bedroom, I opened the clearing house to caregivers and friends. Again everything was gone in a few days.

My clearing house idea was such a hit that my friends wouldn't allow it to end. They brought things they didn't use or want for the clearing house. We store the items in the "Angel's" room (the bedroom Mother and I decorated for our caregivers). A caregiver then places a paper cup on the floor next to the small items for others to put their names in the cup in preparation for a raffle. After all of my caregivers have had a chance to see everything, members of my Spanish family pull the winner's name out of each cup.

Next, we raffle off the donated clothing which has been hung on hangers with a lined paper, a wish list, for people to sign. Sometimes six people sign the list. Of course, only one person can be the winner.

I check each list of names and tell someone in the Spanish group to pick a number from one to the number of names on the list. If there are five names, and number four is chosen, person number four wins the raffle for that item.

The process doesn't take long. The Spanish speaker who pulls the folded names out of the cups or picks the number for the clothing is an impartial person, not me or another caregiver. Items without names are put in a donation box in a nearby shopping center.

Depending upon the number of donations I receive, we schedule a raffle about once a month. Activity associated with the clearing house doesn't take much energy on my part. Considering the positive responses of my caregivers, the organization of the raffle is worth my effort. It appears that my clearing house and raffle have become an institution.

Solving the Vertigo Puzzle

"Whatever you ask for in prayer,
believe that you have received it
and it will be yours."
MARK 11.24 (NIV)

AT THE END OF 2001 I was still trying to resolve some of my health issues, but hadn't fully solved the puzzle they presented. I was experiencing some vertigo attacks, especially in the morning. Javier, my friend who is a physician, suggested that I examine my diet to determine why I still had a problem with vertigo after breakfast. I had eaten my mother's delicious oat muffins almost every day for more than twenty years. Were the muffins causing my vertigo?

To find out I stopped eating the muffins. Evidently I was allergic to oats because when I eliminated the muffins from my diet, I began to feel much better. Javier then recommended that I request blood testing for celiac-sprue. The blood test indicated that I suffered from the disease, which is due to problems associated with the digestion of glutens.

Vickie, a medical librarian who has helped me with research for years, sent me information about celiac-sprue. I began to eliminate glutens from my diet – no more wheat, barley or rye. Oats are only considered a gluten by some nutritionists, but my reaction to eating them was definitely a sign that they were a problem for me. I removed oats from my list of breakfast foods.

My primary physician, Dr. Reimer, then referred me to a gastroenterologist because the ENT (eye, nose and throat doctor) who was following me for the vertigo said I had a reflux disease. Previously, a gastro specialist had said I suffered from Irritable Bowel Syndrome but not reflux. How did the ENT know this without any testing? He said by my "bad breath."

After learning more about the foods that contain gluten, my caregivers, friends and I began reading labels at the grocery store. Many canned goods, soups, and salad dressings had gluten listed as an ingredient. Rice cakes were the only bread exchange that I liked. Later, I found a rice cereal that tasted like Rice Crispies, a favorite breakfast food when I was a child. Trader Joe's brown rice bread became a staple in my diet. Other markets have pastas that are good substitutes for those made with wheat.

Now in 2012, we can find a good selection of gluten-free items in many grocery stores. Our city even has a bakery with many yummy gluten-free baked goods. They are pricey, but I can afford them once in a while.

A series of cookbooks with gluten-free recipes can be found in the library. At this writing you can buy Bisquick's gluten-free mix that makes tasty biscuits and pancakes.

Experimenting with different recipes has become a Sunday adventure for me and my helpers. During the last ten years I have been on the diet, I have had more energy and have maintained my ideal weight. I even enjoy food more now than in former years.

Facing Flames

"For in the day of trouble he will keep me safe..."
PSALM 27.5 (NIV)

FROM THE TIME MOTHER DIED until 2002, my only real problems to be solved were adjusting to my new diet and completing an inventory of my belongings in the house. I felt the need to clean out the condo of many items we hadn't used for years. In the spring of '02 an event occurred which could have been life changing for me.

Except for the garage, the condo attached to mine by a common wall burned to the ground. So many people asked me to relate what happened that I decided to write about the fire and give out copies of my story. Repeating the details about the tragedy was painful. I titled my piece "Facing Flames."

On April 12, 2002, at 1:40 p.m., I sat in my wheelchair at my writing station near the front door. Suddenly, someone began pounding on the double doors as if determined to break them down. Quickly, I pushed my wheelchair close enough to the doors to put on the security lock. I was at home alone.

My caregiver had left just ten minutes earlier. Was it possible that there was someone watching, waiting for her to leave to try to gain entrance to my house? A man yelled, "Your house is on fire!" My smoke alarms had not gone off, and I didn't smell smoke. Was this a trick to get me to unlock the door?

When the person left, he yelled his name. He lived in the condos! I pushed the button on my telephone control, and the operator answered the phone in my bedroom. I shouted, "911! My house is on fire!" Then the smoke alarms began to screech. I had to get out quickly. I unlocked the door, opened it and called, "Someone get me out of the house!"

A young woman I didn't know pulled me into the street to safety. I looked at her quizzically and asked, "Who are you?" She looked like an angel to me. She was Sally, the daughter of my friend, Kirk, who lived at the opposite end of our development. She was walking her mother's dog when she saw the smoke.

As I sat in the road looking at my house and the adjoining unit, I couldn't believe my eyes. Was it a sign? Flames ten feet high were dancing above #102, yet my roof was not burning! There was a distinct separation all the way from the front to the back of the units. My $16,000 *FireFree* roof had saved my life, and probably some of the adjacent units. I would never complain again about the sacrifice I had made to pay for that roof. I felt an inner peace as I etched the image of the units in my memory. But I was thinking, "Is anything burning under my roof?"

During my flight, I had not thought about the way I looked. My hair was wet and in curlers, but fortunately, I was fully dressed. Usually I put on my night gown after my hair was washed. Not that day!

Neighbors were concerned about the occupants of #102. Was anyone asleep and unaware of the fire? Someone among the bystanders said he saw people leave the unit minutes before 1:30 p.m. The man who warned me succeeded in breaking down the door to #102. He had turned off the gas to the units which saved us from an explosion. Others called 911 to report the fire. It seemed like an eternity before the fire engines arrived on the scene.

My wheelchair and I were now in the way. Elaine, a neighbor who had recently moved to a nearby apartment, moved me to the sidewalk where I watched the commotion. She wanted to take me to her home a block away because I was cold and the smoke was thick. But I was expecting a caregiver at 3:00, and she would never find me at this lady's home.

Seven fire trucks lined up with their equipment. The paramedics were also there. Moments later the

Nichols, who lived at the entrance of the condos, arrived after running errands. I asked them if I could come into their unit and make some phone calls. I had to get busy! They invited me in.

First, I called my State Farm Insurance agent, Stuart, and left a message for him describing what was happening.

Then I called Ron, one of my Spanish conversation group members, who agreed to locate my fire and water restoration coordinator, Blair, who was Ron's friend. Blair's company had just completed work in restoring my guest bathroom, hall and south bedrooms that were flooded when a bathtub ran over for hours. The flood originated in the same unit as the fire, #102, adjacent to my home. I had had my beautifully remodeled bathroom merely *one week* before this second tragedy occurred.

I was not surprised that the attached condo burned so quickly. The new owner bought the property "as is" and didn't ask for an inspector's clearance. The roof needed to be replaced and the inside lacked care. It was like a matchbox waiting to explode.

Next, I called my morning helper because I knew she would be needed to move me. But where?

My last call was to my dear friend Carole, who had supported me and Mother during the years of her illness. She didn't answer so I left a message. Later she told me that the minute I pronounced her name she knew something had happened. My tone was "calm and collected," but clearly I was sounding an alarm. The message was: "…This is Susan. I have an emergency. My house is on fire. I am across the street. I need you to come over. Thank you. Good-bye."

The paramedics sent someone to tell me that if I felt any shortness of breath or pain, they were there to help. Thankfully, I did not feel any physical effects of the shock.

Lois, my neighbor who taught me how to make flower cards, became my eyes and ears. Periodically, she entered the Nichol's condo where I was making my calls to describe what was going on outside. The bad news was that the fire fighters decided to tear back my roof to assure them that the fire was not smoldering underneath.

Now that the fire was out, could I re-enter my home where a wall had been removed thirty years ago so that I could use the bathroom? At Lois's insistence the fireman carried me in my chair like a palanquin over their many hoses to enter and find out. The bathroom I used was not damaged.

Due to all the fire trucks, cars, TV news crews and onlookers gathered around the area, my three o'clock helper had to park two blocks away because the street was closed in front of my condo. My morning caregiver was helping me in the bathroom when she arrived.

The Chief of the Fire Department told me that I had to collect my personal belongings and prepare to move immediately. One helper began putting together my special bedding and another started emptying the refrigerator and freezer and putting their contents into boxes.

The electricity was not off long enough to thaw anything so I didn't lose any food. My helpers were going home soon so I could send the food with them and nothing would spoil. While I was directing their work, Diane, a resident of the condos, whom I had only met once before, arrived to offer her home as a temporary refuge. I accepted this "angel's" gracious offer with relief thinking I could manage for one night using my portable toilet until I could move into a motel.

After Carole arrived, she sat in the kitchen near the open door to answer the phone while we worked. Because the smoke was visible for miles, people were calling to ask if I was OK.

When we had carried my things to Diane's unit, I was delighted to find out that with some maneuvering, my night helper Lisa, who was thin, could transfer me on to the toilet. The bedroom was also large enough so that I could transfer into and out of bed in my usual way.

People came and went: Stuart, my insurance agent and longtime friend, and his adjuster; David, my CPA who corrected an error on my income tax form which was due on the following Monday, three days later.

Aimee, a retired helper had called in the morning because she had felt the urge to visit me that day. When she arrived at the condo, she couldn't believe the fire scene and asked neighbors what had happened to ME. They directed her to Diane's condo, my temporary refuge. By then, there were many people coming and going at my new home. I was exhausted but grateful for all of the people who demonstrated their love that day. How blessed I was during the whole experience!

The State Farm insurance adjuster, who had covered my water damage, suggested that I call a residence inn and move there the next day. He gave me a generous advance. Later I called the inn and made an appointment to check out their rooms in the morning.

That night Lisa slept on the floor of my room because the monitor we use to connect our rooms would not work. I rested, prayed and listened for answers.

*"Therefore do not worry about tomorrow,
for tomorrow will worry about itself.
Each day has enough trouble of its own."*
Matthew 6.34 (NIV)

In the morning, I felt a "nudge" to call the apartments located at the mouth of our condo entrance. At 7:15 a.m. I phoned their office and asked if they had a vacancy. Yes, they did! The manager knew about the fire and said I could come at nine to see if I could use the bathroom in their two bedroom unit. I couldn't!

Jerry, my adopted "son," who helps me on Saturday mornings, took off the bathroom door in the apartment. Now my chair could enter the room, but there wasn't space enough to turn it toward the toilet. I asked whether the bathrooms were the same in all units. I had such a strong feeling that I was supposed to be housed there.

The manager, Blanche, told us that they had a three bedroom house at the end of the complex that was empty. But she thought the units' bathrooms were all the same. We went to the house to check it out.

On the outside the house looked as if it had been abandoned for a long time. The inside was an answer to my prayers. It was a "Mansion."

The bathroom was a dream! Big enough to turn around in a circle once inside the wide door. I rented the house immediately. My helpers could push me to my condo when I had to be there. Again God had provided for my needs.

"And God is faithful;
he will not let you be tempted
beyond what you can bear.
But when you are tempted,
he will also provide a way out
so that you can stand up under it."
1 CORINTHIANS 10.13 (NIV)

Over the weekend we returned to see the damage that had been done to my unit. The walls and ceilings of the rooms that are joined to unit #102 by the fire wall were burned. The bathroom was completely destroyed according to those who looked at it. I decided that it was best for me not to see that area of the house as I was having enough problems sleeping. Seeing the destruction there would have contributed to my nightmares.

The fire had entered through the bathroom skylight. If Keo, my Asian caregiver, had not closed the bathroom door in the afternoon as was the custom in her native country, the whole house would have been burned. The door acted as a protective fire wall.

A caregiver and her husband moved some of my clothes that were not soiled to the residence inn where we rested until Monday. Saturday and Sunday Blanche and her daughter cleaned the house.

Early Monday morning we began to move with the help of many friends and Blair's restoration crew of eight people. In two days we were settled in the new house. I only lost the contents of my newly decorated bathroom. Two living room chairs needed recovering. They had everything else cleaned in three weeks. With pictures hung in place I felt comfortable in my new home. The Village Readers even met there on schedule.

After we were settled, Blanche and I discussed our feelings about my experience. The "Mansion" had been empty for more than a month, but she was not motivated to clean it up for rental. She agreed that I could stay there as long as I needed to. Had the Lord prepared this place for me? I think so.

The "Mansion" had 2,200 square feet. Everything but my refrigerator was stored there, mostly in boxes waiting to be moved back after reconstruction of the units.

One drawback of the house was that I had to have twenty-four hour care there, seven more hours than usual. I couldn't move on the thick carpet nor open any of the doors leading to the outside. My personal insurance adjuster agreed to pay for the additional care I needed.

My caregivers expanded their shifts to accommodate me. I prayed that as their school schedules changed, they could still help me. I knew God was in charge of my situation, and I waited with hope for the day I could return to my beautiful, convenient home.

"Morning by morning, O Lord,
you hear my voice;
morning by morning
I lay my requests before you
and wait in expectation."
Psalm 5.3 (NIV)

Living through a Nightmare

"Hear my prayer, O God;
listen to the words of my mouth."
PSALM 54.2 (NIV)

A FEW DAYS AFTER THE FIRE, I learned that the owner of #102 did not have insurance to cover the damage inside her unit. During the first week when I was outside in my front patio, she came to my gate and asked where I was living. I told her about my first night at a neighbor's condo and related the answer to my prayer, a place nearby. How grateful I was to be so close to Village Gardens. She said she had called there and the rent was very high.

Later, I heard that one of the Villagers was collecting money to help her. I told my dear friend Jane that if anyone wanted to do something for me, instead of money I hoped she'd suggest that I would like a small box of four or five impatiens plants. I wanted to fill the barren back patio that was outside a full-length glass kitchen door. In a few days many colorful flowers covered the space. It was beginning to feel like home.

Another neighbor, Kirk, who was a prominent artist in town, brought many spider plants of various sizes to decorate the front patio. With the green and white stripes and a few potted rose bushes loaned by a close friend, Virginia, the beautifully landscaped entrance looked like the house had been inhabited for years.

After I settled down in my new home, the Village Garden Board, the insurance adjusters for the condo, and the representative for the insurance company from San Francisco, who was charged with the renovations, began their calculations.

As I started to write about the time it took to struggle with them to receive what was needed to bring my home up to the standard it was before the fire, I felt the same stress I endured at the beginning of the process. It was like living through my worst nightmare again.

Without the Psalms I couldn't have faced each day. I was at the brink of exploding every time I had to justify why something had to be done or done correctly.

"In your anger do not sin;
when you are on your beds,
search your hearts and be silent."
PSALM 4.4 (NIV)

I started collecting memos I wrote before renovation even began. They filled three thick files. I never went through anything as horrible before or after that period of my life. The negative experiences I encountered tested my ability to control my anger and frustration. Fortunately, I felt the Lord beside me during many confrontations with some of the people associated with my claim.

I wasn't sleeping well. Villagers kept remarking about how well I looked and how they couldn't have held up through all that was happening. I knew the Lord was calming me. My nightly repetitions of two phrases are still etched on my brain; "Be still, and know that I am God" and "This too will pass."

"Wait for the Lord;
be strong and take heart
and wait for the Lord."
PSALM 27.14 (NIV)

After the asbestos clearance, work began on #102. To save money, when a crew came to work on a certain aspect both the units needed, they spent time in both of them. But because most of the structure of my unit was not damaged, there were days and weeks when they didn't work on it.

Keeping Busy at the Mansion

EVEN THOUGH THE ELECTRICITY WAS turned off at my house, we were able to use the sprinklers on manual. Every other day I went with one of my caregivers to run the sprinklers enough to keep the "back 40" and the bushes and flowers in the front patio alive. We didn't want my home to appear abandoned when I wasn't there.

With the outside watering being tended, we began to plan what we could do inside the apartment when finished with our chores.

We stored the furniture we weren't using in the empty master bedroom. There was lots of space for storage and a work area. We began by setting up "stations" where we could work on projects. First, a computer station was arranged. We began to compile a notebook of friends' current addresses.

I had always wanted to type Mother's recipes and collate them in a large notebook. Now we had time to accomplish this task.

As my bedding, clothes and other items were returned after being cleaned, I began to think about what our next projects would be.

My personal belongings and wood furniture came through the cleaning better than I expected. The living room and two southern bedroom drapes had to be replaced. My bedroom drapes looked like new after being cleaned. I made an appointment with a person who would make customized drapes for the living room and bedrooms.

I had decided I wanted to design a new look for the kitchen where I spent many happy hours. The large kitchen drape had been in a sunny area for twenty years. I knew it would never hold up through a cleaning. I asked for the cost of cleaning it in cash. Fortunately, it was ninety dollars. This was enough to pay for material to make a valence to hang over the large glass door and window, a Roman shade for the side window and a large cork board covered with matching material as a wall hanging.

We began to shop for material: bright cotton floral for the kitchen and durable upholstery fabric for the living room chairs. We found the floral first and the caregivers began measuring, cutting and pinning it on the floor of the work room. None of that was a favorite job for one of my caregivers. Otherwise, I didn't hear any complaints or groaning from the others. I think they were excited about seeing our work in the kitchen when we could move back to my home.

Our next shopping trip was to find the fabric to cover the chairs. The main fabric store in town was having a terrific sale. The price of what I liked was so reasonable that I bought enough to have the dining chairs covered and pay for the work myself. Mother had always wanted to cover the living and dining chairs with matching fabric. We often used these chairs together when we entertained large groups. I could feel Mother's nudge to make this possible. I'm sure she was smiling in Heaven to know we would finally make her dream come true.

Because I couldn't work on the floor or pin large pieces of material together, I wanted another station nearby in the room where I could supervise the preparation of the components for the kitchen. We put together a flower station where I could make cards for the people who had been so generous with us during the move and landscaping of the patios.

We still had to find a drape or drapes for the kitchen. JCPenney had exactly what we needed, white cotton panels that could completely or partially close out the light or darkness. Our needs were met, one by one and our hearts were singing.

"Count your many blessings,
Name them one by one.
Count your blessings;
See what God hath done.
Name them one by one."
(COUNT YOUR BLESSINGS,
OATMAN & EXCELL, 1972)

We were going to be ready when given the all clear to move back home.

Going Home

MOVING BACK TO MY CONDO was an event to celebrate. I quickly reverted to my old routine.

I found the eight large boxes that contained my HOPE pamphlets intact. They were in the heavily smoked bedroom. I think putting ten each in plastic bags had saved them. A miracle? I think so.

All paintings and flower pictures had been restored. The furniture in the bedrooms cleaned up well. With everything placed differently in all the rooms, the house seemed to have more space and was much brighter.

After we put everything we made for the kitchen in place, I sewed ties for the drapes out of the flowered material. The yellow upholstered kitchen chairs were the finishing touch for a bright kitchen. I made the chairs "child proof" by covering them with clear plastic. I wanted little ones to enjoy eating at my house without fearing spills.

Now I began to make cards to sell at the annual Kappa Alpha Theta boutique. I also sold my pamphlets there. I asked my friend Lois, who taught me how to make the flower cards, to sell hers there too.

Soon after that Lois became very ill with cancer. The doctor restricted her visitors and phone calls to conserve her strength.

She was in my thoughts and prayers 24/7. I kept finding prayers and scriptures that I thought would comfort her. Was there a way to share these with her? Sure! The answer was to type them out and place one in her mailbox each day. For 60 days one of my caregivers put my typed messages in her box.

Then Lois was moved to her daughter's home in another city for her last days. Sharon, one of my caregivers who had also worked with Lois for several years, suggested that I combine some of these messages in another HOPE pamphlet. She helped me put together *Facing Life's Trials with HOPE*. The attractive title has appealed to many people and now is the most popular of the series.

I will always be grateful to Lois, a loving Christian friend, who encouraged me to share my love of flowers in the cards I give to my loved ones and friends on special occasions.

> *"Then sings my soul, my Savior God to Thee.*
> *How great Thou art, how great Thou art!"*
> **(HOW GREAT THOU ART. BOBERG, 1972)**

Enduring the "Golden Years"

"Therefore we do not lose heart.
Though outwardly we are wasting away,
yet inwardly we are being renewed day by day."
2 CORINTHIANS 4.16 (NIV)

I BEGAN NOTING CHANGES IN MY physical condition after the fire. Were they due to aging or associated with the symptoms of the post-polio syndrome (PPS) or both? How was I to tell the difference?

The circulation in my legs had *always* been affected, but I was able to sit comfortably for many hours. When in my home again after the fire, I began to be uncomfortable when I sat for only three or four hours. My right personal "cushion" was noticeably red, especially after working at the computer. I did not want to be bed bound with breakdown of my skin.

"In the day of my trouble I will call to you,
for you will answer me."
PSALM 86.7 (NIV)

I called my doctor and requested an examination by a wound care specialist. The nurse who came thought I had become aware of my symptoms sufficiently early to avoid a serious problem. She recommended a different wheelchair cushion and suggested that I start on an oxygen regimen which is important to healthy skin.

My breathing was becoming shallower. This was definitely associated with the PPS. A study of my breathing pattern showed a significant decline in capacity since my last test in the '80s. I had been yawning a lot during the evening. After I began to use the oxygen, I noticed an increase in energy during the evening hours and less yawning.

As time passed, the lack of adequate circulation in my legs became more of a problem. I was always cold. My extremities that were not paralyzed became weaker (PPS), especially my left arm.

I noticed that my balance was causing me problems, so much so that one person using a sliding board could no longer transfer me from chair to car safely. I was beginning to lose the strength I built up after polio rehabilitation. Retirement reduced my movement and lessened my exercise time. Recently, I added a "push myself" time during the evening news which I pray will help me maintain strength.

Many other seniors were falling and breaking bones due to balance problems. So far I haven't broken any bones. This surprises me because a physician, reviewing my chest x-rays taken in 1984, said that my ribs were like tissue paper.

My wrinkles, thinning hair, unwanted facial hair and other aging changes are unavoidable signs that I have lived with for many years. Maintaining a smile on my face and a song in my heart demonstrate that the years have passed without destroying my positive attitude.

How was I to forge ahead, wrinkles, wild untidy hair, scoliosis and all?

God had plans for me. I just had to wait for His direction. It would come in His timing. I tried to wait patiently for the sign. It came in 2011 through Maxine, my neighbor.

"Lead me, O Lord, in your righteousness…
make straight your way before me."
PSALM 5.8 (NIV)

Helping Seniors and the Disabled

A FTER MOTHER'S DEATH IN '95 I had evaluated my situation. I asked myself if I should try to stay at home alone. I knew I would be happiest if I remained where I had lived for twenty-two years.

Because I didn't have family in Fresno, I began to develop a "family" with the trustworthy and responsible caregivers who were with me during Mother's illness; those who felt like family to both of us.

From 1995 until 2012, I lived independently in my home with the help of these people and other caregivers. Many of my neighbors, who are also seniors, watched my life revolve smoothly even though I am confined to a wheelchair and totally dependent upon others for my care. Some had called to ask whether any of my helpers could work for them. I enjoyed sharing what I had learned with others.

In 2011, Maxine called and asked if I would talk with Mary, one of her friends. Mary's husband faced an amputation, a crippling crisis. She didn't know how she was going to care for him at home. Would I talk with her about how I've managed to live alone? Of course, I would.

At the end of our conversation, Maxine suggested that I write down my method of finding and keeping such wonderful caregivers. She had read an easy to read book by Barbara Feldon titled *Living Alone & Loving It* that helped her when she experienced lonely times in her life. She suggested that I share my knowledge about hiring caregivers with others in a similar book with a step-by-step format. Was this the answer to my prayer that I'd been waiting for?

I asked myself, Did I have energy enough to begin the project? As always, I prayed and soon received my answer. It was in 1 Peter 4.10 (NIV):

> *"Each one should use whatever gifts*
> *he has received to serve others…"*

I knew I should have a goal to be serving others in God's name. I had several talented caregivers who could help me with the secretarial tasks that required me to sit long hours at the computer. I began outlining chapter headings and putting forms that I used into an appendix. My suggestions would be directed to (1) seniors and the disabled who don't have someone to care for their needs at certain times of the day and/

or night, and (2) people who live on a fixed income, which is sufficient to cover ordinary expenses but too much to receive governmental support, and who have some savings for emergencies.

Unfortunately, a large group of elders fits into the last category. They receive a monthly pension and Social Security, yet they couldn't afford to pay for the amount of caregiver hours they need through an agency. I certainly couldn't.

When I had a rough draft of the manuscript completed, I asked my friends Jane and Bette (a book publisher) to read what I'd put together. I also wanted suggestions for a title.

At first I thought of *The Source* because that was what I wanted the book to be, a source for helping people find caregivers. Nobody liked that title.

Both reviewers thought I should include two more chapters, one about why I needed care providers and the other to explain how I had achieved my goal to become a professor at a university. Because Mother and I often referred to the helpers as our angels and the room where they rested and slept as the angels' room, my friend Jane thought that *House of Angels* was a perfect title. I did, too.

Susan surrounded by the "angels" who
took care of her in 2011-2012.

Now I had to find a publisher. I contacted the printer who had worked with me to print my HOPE pamphlets at a reasonable price. He agreed to help me as I learned about the publishing business. He wanted to buy a new machine which would cut printing costs considerably.

After I read many books about publishing, I decided self-publishing, with the printer's assistance, was the way to go. At 81 years of age I didn't have the time nor the funds to search for a publisher.

By 2011, I had sold over 10,000 of the HOPE series to hospices in twenty-one states. Due to rising postal rates and declining donations to hospices, I stopped sending sample copies of the pamphlets to hospices in other cities. Hospice Care of California has continued to buy 100 copies of *Facing Life's Trials with HOPE* every three or four months. By 2012 the total sold had increased to 12,000. Sharon, the caregiver who inspired me to collect prayers and scripture for *Facing Life's Trials*, wants to continue with this ministry when I no longer can manage it.

With thoughts of my success putting thousands of pamphlets in the hands of people who needed HOPE, I was encouraged to look for the best way to continue working on *House of Angels*. Surely there was an economical way to get my text on the market. This was the year the baby boomers came of age (65) and the need for caregivers would increase.

Getting Joyful News

As I waited for the book to be in final form I received an interesting call from Paul Ogden, a colleague at Fresno State. The University was preparing for the 100 year anniversary of its existence. The faculty was reviewing lists of retired professors. My name was on the list but there was no mention of my emeritus status. Those present at the meeting thought that was an error. Paul, who had been there during my tenure, explained the situation to the group. I had not been nominated for the honor.

Those present decided to nominate me. The faculty wanted to surprise me, but I had to be involved because I needed to put together a résumé.

This presented a problem. When I was 75, I destroyed the papers I thought I'd never need in the future. I only kept the eight-page list of my publications. It was impressive, but there were more items I needed to include.

My first step was to call the offices which had, on file, the dates of my service on various committees. I couldn't remember the dates of my chairmanship of the department so I had to check into the archives to find the information. My California Speech-Language Association honors were easy to remember.

Now I had to wait until Andrew Hoff, the Dean of the College of Health and Human Services, signed my papers. I was told he was very supportive of the department's request. The last step was the approval of the University's President Welty. The congratulatory letter with his signature came two weeks before my book went to press. This was in time for my honor to be included on my biography page and in the Foreword written by my friend Bob Calmes, M.D., a neurologist who had taught in the department when I was chair.

"I will deliver him and honor him."
PSALM 91.14-15 (NIV)

Marketing *House of Angels*

IN AUGUST 2011, COPIES OF the book were available to sell. I began the most difficult job for me – MARKETING. How could I get the book into the hands of my projected audience? I wanted to help Fresno seniors and the disabled who were looking for caregivers.

Each day I focused on the prayer of Jabez believing that if I truly had been led to write *House of Angels*, in God's time the book would begin to sell.

"Jabez cried out to the God of Israel,
'Oh that you would bless me and enlarge my territory!
Let your hand be with me..."'
1 CHRONICLES 4.10 (NIV)

At the beginning of the University fall session, Dean Hoff included a picture of the book cover and a short announcement about the book on the welcoming section of the college website. Susan, the manager of the Fresno State Kennel Book Store agreed to place copies on their faculty shelf.

I wanted a placement where many seniors frequented. Would the owner of a pharmacy where Mother went for her weekly blood pressure reading put the book in her gift area? She had put some of my HOPE pamphlets there in the past. She said YES.

With the book in convenient places I was ready to call the Senior Living editor of the Fresno Bee and ask for coverage of my new book to help other seniors. To my surprise, she sent a person to interview me and a photographer to my home several days later.

The Bee coverage was great; a two-page spread with two photos. They also included information about the HOPE series of pamphlets and my flower cards.

People who didn't know I was writing a book started calling me. Many went to buy the book where it was available. Coordinators for three branches of Fresno's libraries called me to schedule presentations for their patrons.

Unfortunately, Borders Bookstore and our neighborhood Fig Garden Book Store closed in 2011. The manager of the Fresno Barnes and Noble store referred me to their Small Press Department coordinator in New York. I was told that they did not want to place the book in the store but would list it on their website. I began this process in September of 2011 and the listing appeared on the website just before I submitted *Chosen…To Never Walk Alone!* to Inspiring Voices.

I wanted to have a book signing in Fresno as soon as possible. The manager of the local Berean Christian Store encouraged me by scheduling a signing in April. The Bee's religious editor announced the signing with a short description of the book.

The people who came to the signing included old friends, a student who was in one of my classes in the '80s and a former aphasic patient who had a remarkable recovery after receiving therapy at the University Language, Speech and Hearing Clinic. It was a pleasant experience.

In November of 2012, Barnes and Noble included pictures of the front and back covers of *House of Angels* on their website and requested readers to submit comments about the book. I was surprised to find my biography and a description of the book, including a table of contents and appendices on their website. I anxiously awaited my first order from them.

Receiving an Answer to Prayer

"For everyone who asks receives;
he who seeks finds;
and to him who knocks,
the door will be opened."
Luke 11.10 (NIV)

FRIENDS WHO KNEW MY DESIRE to find ways to market in Fresno came up with some ideas I might try. My friend Midge called to tell me about a church sponsored conference focusing on caregiving and facing the changes in life styles associated with aging. This seemed to be a perfect place to sell my book.

I quickly contacted the person in charge for information about becoming a vendor. My call was a day late for registering. Fortunately, the lady who answered my call offered to put a flyer about *House of Angels* inside their program if I would immediately send her a description of the book, places where it could be purchased, and any other pertinent information.

When I arrived on the day of the workshops, Judy, the lady I had talked with, who was a coordinator of the event, had forgotten to bring the flyers. She immediately ran out of the church explaining that she left the flyers at home and would be right back with them.

During the initial announcements Judy explained that my page should have appeared in the program and would be available at a nearby table. I was impressed by her gesture of Christian love.

But this was not the answer to prayer I was waiting for. My prayer of many months had to do with my physical condition and transportation problems.

Since selling my car, I had begun to use public transportation. There was a Fresno bus that picked me up at home and took me and my caregivers to any place in the city. But they would not cross over the city boundaries.

My doctor's office was located in Clovis, which had its own bus system. To get there I would have to transfer from the Fresno bus to the Clovis bus. At 81 years old I knew this was not an option for me.

Although I was satisfied with my doctor's care, I shared my problem with him and prayed to find a doctor in Fresno.

The first workshop I attended at the caregivers' conference was titled "The Doctor Is In." I was impressed with the doctors' answers to questions asked by the participants, especially by the internist,

Dr. Gong, who was associated with a well-respected medical group in Fresno.

As everyone began to leave, I motioned to Dr. Gong and said I'd like to talk with him. I told him about my transportation problem and asked if he would be my doctor. He said "yes," gave me his card, and told me to make an appointment soon.

I was so excited I wanted to share this news with Judy, my new "sister in Christ." She told me he was her doctor and also that he wasn't taking new patients – but he took ME.

A week later I made our first appointment, wrote a letter to my Clovis doctor thanking him for his care and asked that he send the most important information in my file to Dr. Gong, my new doctor.

During our initial appointment, I was impressed with Dr. Gong's manner and convinced that I was where I should be. This experience was an unexpected answer to my prayers. Set up by God? I think so!

"…Is anyone happy?
Let him sing songs of praise."
JAMES 5.13 (NIV)

Accepting a Surprising Call

FOR THIRTY-NINE YEARS TWO SISTERS in Toledo, OH have published a magazine about the historic Maumee Valley which includes Toledo, Maumee, Perrysburg and other cities surrounding the Maumee River. They call it *Bend of the River*. Through the years several of my friends from Toledo who receive the magazine have given me a subscription to the publication.

When I began marketing *House of Angels*, Nancy Campbell, a high school and Michigan State Theta friend who lives in Phoenix and corresponds with me regularly, asked my permission to send an article about me to the *Bend*. Nancy's aim was to describe my accomplishments since contracting polio in 1949. Of course, she wanted to include information to help me market the book.

I sent Nancy several pictures because they always include black and white photos with an article, if possible. In April they published a two column spread titled "1948 DeVilbiss Grad Overcomes Obstacles" with my senior yearbook picture.

In April, before Nancy and I received our copies, she called to ask my permission to give my phone number to one of our classmates, Jim Crumley, who lives in Toledo. He had already received his April copy of the magazine and thought Nancy had done a good job presenting my story. Jim said he had a surprise for me. I told Nancy I'd be happy to hear from him. I wondered what the surprise was.

When Jim called, he began to tell an almost unbelievable story. He said one of his favorite pastimes was to browse in used bookstores and see what they had of interest. Recently, he found a 1946 Pot-of-Gold, the yearbook of our high school. His picture as a track star and mine were in it.

At the end of the book, there were several pages of messages written by schoolmates to someone named Susie. He wondered who the Susie was they were referencing. Then he came across a message that mentioned a party the writer attended in Michigan. Jim had also gone to a party at my place in Michigan. Then right away he knew, I was that Susie! It was *my* yearbook.

I was truly amazed! How did the yearbook find its way back to me? Where had it been since 1960 when I gave the book away during preparations to move to Arizona? Mother wanted me to keep all three of my

DeVilbiss yearbooks when we moved, but I decided to only keep my senior book. I was very active that year and there were many pictures of me in it.

Had Mother led my friend to the bookstore where my book was housed? Of course, I may never know the answer to this question or how the book got back to me.

Several weeks later Jim sent the book to me in the mail. I have enjoyed looking through it and remembering the friends I met during my first year at DeVilbiss.

Nancy was disappointed because the editors of the *Bend* removed the section about *House of Angels*. The magazine's editor explained that they sell ads and for this reason never include anything that could be considered an ad in articles. As Mother would have said, "You can't win them all."

Taking the Book on the Road

"For God did not give us a spirit of timidity,
but a spirit of power..."
2 TIMOTHY 1.7 (NIV)

BEFORE SCHEDULING PUBLIC PRESENTATIONS OF *House of Angels*, I had to consider which highlights to include. First, I had to establish my credibility as an author of a book about caregivers.

I looked for data. How many caregivers had I employed? My assistant collated the annual lists of my caregivers and found 115 on the lists from 1992 until 2011. This did not include students who were paid through Friendly Visitors, a Fresno State caregiver program. I only let two of the 115 go who did not meet my standards. Most had been a blessing to Mother and me.

I was nervous about speaking in public. I hadn't spoken to a large group since I retired from teaching in 1992. Could I still present the book so that people would see how useful it was for anyone looking for caregivers? The words above from 2nd Timothy gave me courage.

Melanie, my assistant, produced a PowerPoint presentation to accompany my talk and help to hold the interest of my audience.

The thirty minute talk was to be followed by a question and answer period for about fifteen minutes. I hoped to sell and autograph books after my talk.

Melanie and I were now ready to begin our marketing adventure. My friends continued to suggest ways I could reach more audiences.

Resting through the Summer

"Come to me, all you who are weary...
and I will give you rest."
MATTHEW 11.28 (NIV)

I DID NOT SCHEDULE ANY PRESENTATIONS of *House of Angels* during the summer of 2012. I still had to rest after two or three hours in my chair to avoid advancing my Stage 1 pressure areas to Stage 2. The red areas, typical of Stage 1, begin to ulcerate in Stage 2.

On June 12th I was fitted for a new wheelchair which would be designed to help me sit more comfortably. The salesman, who was highly recommended by two retired physical therapists, told me Medicare would pay for it.

At home I was still using the small chair that I was given in 1950 by the March of Dimes. It weighs 54 pounds.

In 1960 I bought a lighter chair that weighed 32 pounds, when I began working in Phoenix. Mother couldn't continue lifting the old chair in and out of the car every day. When in Ohio, my male caregivers transported me to the University of Toledo and Bowling Green. They could easily lift the heavy chair in and out of the trunk. Now we could leave the new light chair in the trunk of the car and have it available when Mother had to lift it. I continued to use the old one at home.

In 1970 when I started teaching in Fresno, I purchased a motorized chair to become independent on campus. It wore out in 1992, just before I retired. Rick, a student's husband, who kept it in repair all those years, could no longer replace worn parts.

I am hopeful that the new chair will be more comfortable and will allow me to sit for longer periods of time. In November 2012 I plan to begin scheduling more presentations of *House of Angels* in the community. I pray that the summer rest will have prepared me for the longer hours needed to hit the marketing road again.

Traveling Forward

LIKE MY MOTHER, I HOPE to focus the rest of my life on Psalm 23.

> *"Surely goodness and love will follow me*
> *all the days of my life,..."*
> **PSALM 23.6 (NIV)**

I continue to live with the warmth of the promise in the last words of the Psalm.

> *"...and I will dwell*
> *in the house*
> *of the Lord forever."*
> **PSALM 23.6 (NIV)**

I may have a long or short road to travel. Whatever happens in the future, I hope to run my race...

> *"Forgetting what is behind and*
> *straining toward what is ahead."*
> **PHILIPPIANS 3.13 (NIV)**

I am thankful for past opportunities for growth and am grateful for those who have supported me on my walk.

I've never had to walk alone.

Bibliography of Lyrics/Hymns

Boberg, Carl, "How Great Thou Art," Number 5 in <u>Worship in Song: Nazarene Hymnal</u>, Kansas City, MO: Lillenas Publishing Co., 1972.

Brown, Mary & Rounsefell, Carrie E., "I'll Go Where You Want Me to Go," Number 354 in <u>Worship in Song: Nazarene Hymnal</u>, Kansas City, MO: Lillenas Publishing Co., 1972.

Chisholm, Thomas O., & Runyan, William M., "Great is Thy Faithfulness," Number 86 in <u>Worship in Song: Nazarene Hymnal</u>, Kansas City, MO: Lillenas Publishing Co., 1972.

Crosby, Fanny J., & Doane, W. H., "To God Be the Glory," Number 3 in <u>Worship in Song: Nazarene Hymnal</u>, Kansas City, MO: Lillenas Publishing Co., 1972.

Elliott, Charlotte & Bradbury, William B., "Just As I Am," Number 232 in <u>Worship in Song: Nazarene</u>

Hymnal, Kansas City, MO: Lillenas Publishing Co., 1972.

Green, Bud; Brown, Les; & Homer, Ben, "Sentimental Journey." Sentimental Journey performed by David Rose and His Orchestra, MGM Records, 1956.

Hammerstein II, Oscar & Rogers, Richard, "You'll Never Walk Alone," In Rogers and Hammerstein Song Book, New York: Simon and Schuster and Williamson Music, Inc., 1968.

Harris W. J. & Young, V., "Sweet Sue, Just You," Introduced by Sue Carrol, performed by Ben Pollack & Orchestra, 1928, Revival recording #1 by Mills Bros., 1932, Tommy Dorsey & Orchestra, 1939, Johnny Long & Orchestra, 1949.

Hawthorne, Alice, "Whispering Hope," In Country & Western Gospel Hymnal, Grand Rapids, MI: Songsperation Music, 1972.

Ken, Thomas & Bourgeois, Louis, "Praise God from Whom All Blessings Flow," Back cover of Worship in Song: Nazarene Hymnal, Kansas City, MO: Lillenas Publishing Co., 1972.

Martin, Civilla D. & Gabriel, Charles II., "His Eye is on the Sparrow," 1905.

McCarthy, Joseph & Tierney, Harry, "Alice Blue Gown," 1919.

Oatman, Johnson & Excell, Edwin, "Count Your Blessings," Number 89 in Worship in Song: Nazarene Hymnal, Kansas City, MO: Lillenas Publishing Co., 1972.

Pollard, Adelaide A., & Stebbins, George C., "Have Thine Own Way, Lord," Number 276 in Worship in Song: Nazarene Hymnal, Kansas City, MO: Lillenas Publishing Co., 1972.

Sandell-Berg, Carolina V., & Ahnfelt, Oskar, "Day By Day," Number 61 in Worship in Song: Nazarene Hymnal, Kansas City, MO: Lillenas Publishing Co., 1972.

Shanks, Susan J., & Ude, William R., "Be My Guide," 1982.

Spafford, Horatio G., & Bliss, Phillip P., "It is Well with My Soul," Number 70 in <u>Worship in Song: Nazarene Hymnal</u>, Kansas City, MO: Lillenas Publishing Co., 1972.

Meditations

written by Susan J. Shanks
that appeared in
El Aposento Alto (The Upper Room)

Ni la muerte nos separará (Not Even Death Will Separate Us), *El Aposento Alto*, 1-14-90, pg. 21.

Una vara de apoyo (A Supporting Rod), *El Aposento Alto*, 2-23-93, pg. 59.

Una manera de testificar (A Way to Testify), *El Aposento Alto*, June 1997, pg. 12.

Ansiedad sobre el futuro (Anxiety about the Future), *El Aposento Alto*, September/October 2000, pg. 64.

¿Está preso? (Are you in Prison?), *El Aposento Alto*, May/June 2001, pg. 59.

Herido por nuestros pecados (Wounded by our Sins), *El Aposento Alto*, March/April 2005, pg. 13.